VOCAL COSMETICS

(A Complete Package of Vocabulary Usage for IELTS)

Jyoti Malhotra
(B.A Hons. M.A., NET-1, E-Commerce)

Published by:

F-2/16, Ansari road, Daryaganj, New Delhi-110002
☎ 23240026, 23240027 • *Fax:* 011-23240028
info@vspublishers.com • www.vspublishers.com

Online Brandstore: amazon.in/vspublishers

Regional Office : Hyderabad
5-1-707/1, Brij Bhawan (Beside Central Bank of India Lane)
Bank Street, Koti, Hyderabad - 500 095
☎ 040-24737290
vspublishershyd@gmail.com

Follow us on:   

BUY OUR BOOKS FROM: AMAZON FLIPKART

ISBN 978-93-505712-7-9
New Edition

DISCLAIMER

While every attempt has been made to provide accurate and timely information in this book, neither the author nor the publisher assumes any responsibility for errors, unintended omissions or commissions detected therein. The author and publisher makes no representation or warranty with respect to the comprehensiveness or completeness of the contents provided.

All matters included have been simplified under professional guidance for general information only, without any warranty for applicability on an individual. Any mention of an organization or a website in the book, by way of citation or as a source of additional information, doesn't imply the endorsement of the content either by the author or the publisher. It is possible that websites cited may have changed or removed between the time of editing and publishing the book.

Results from using the expert opinion in this book will be totally dependent on individual circumstances and factors beyond the control of the author and the publisher.

It makes sense to elicit advice from well informed sources before implementing the ideas given in the book. The reader assumes full responsibility for the consequences arising out from reading this book.

For proper guidance, it is advisable to read the book under the watchful eyes of parents/guardian. The buyer of this book assumes all responsibility for the use of given materials and information.

Printed at : Param Offsetters, Okhla, New Delhi–110020

Dedication

I, with due respect and profound privilege, serene dignity and folded hands dedicate my small piece of research program to my devoted and dedicated parents, Mrs. Kiran Malhotra and Mr. Pradeep Malhotra for their wholesome support and their dignified ambience which they offered me to sail the boat of my life on the path of hardwork and determination. I am really very thankful to both of them for blooming my life with their humble ambience.

Dedication

I with due respect and profound privilege, serene dignity and folded hands dedicate my small piece of research program to my devoted and dedicated parents, Mrs. Kiran Malhotra and Mr. Pradeep Malhotra for their wholesome support and their dignified guidance which they offered me to sail the boat of my life on the path of hardwork and determination. I am really very thankful to both of them for blooming my life with their humble ambience.

Acknowledgement

There is a big vote bank of thanks in my whole projection of this project to my worthy parents, Mrs. & Mr. Deep Birla, My Guide, Mr. Parminder Singh Bhogal, Caring Brothers & Sisters - Mrs. & Mr. Rohit Gandhi, Mrs. & Mr. Aman Malhotra and Mrs. & Mr. Sandeep Malhotra.

My heartiest thanks to my life partner, Mr. Deepak Malhotra (husband) and the little steps of my Angel, Ditya Malhotra (daughter).

I am really grateful to be a part of the V & S Publishers who support my research analysis with their expert team of publishing. I am really very thankful to Mr. Sahil Gupta (Director) and Mr. Binay Srivastava for their wholesome cooperation to convert my research program to a complete masterpiece.

Regards

Jyoti Malhotra

Publisher's Note

V&S Publishers has recently ventured into the field of *Academic Books* with the launch of the *Gen X Series*. 'Gen X' stands for 'Excellence in Generation 'X'. The series comprises books for aspirants of various competitive examinations. Hence, following the success of our previous books in this series, we decided to launch a **series of IELTS or the International English Language Testing System books** under this series. The subject has been divided into five main parts which has been grouped into five books by the author, such as: ***IELTS Tech-Academic Module***, ***IELTS Tech-Writing Essentials***, ***IELTS Tech-Vocal Cosmetics***, ***IELTS Tech- General Module*** and ***IELTS Tech- Speaking Essentials*** for the students, who aspire to study, work or settle abroad.

The books in this exclusive Series are written especially for the Indian students who wish to appear in the IELTS exams. Most of the foreign books available in the market on this subject have been written keeping in view the foreign readers and at times, may appear *Greek* to the students from India, primarily because of issues related to accent, grammatical aspects, spellings, etc. Therefore, the need for these books was felt by V&S Publishers and the author's extensive research on this subject was carefully moulded to present it in the form of five perfect books on IELTS, specifically for Indian students.

Each book contains **Skills, Strategies and Guidelines** written in a simple manner along with a CD that accompanies the book which is also one of the unique features of this Series. The **CDs are interactive and illustrative** and presented in a manner that even an average student can grasp the contents and master the language easily and quickly. So, V&S Publishers hopes that through these books, we can offer the IELTS aspirants--**A Smarter Way to Learn Technical English nationwide.**

Contents

Preface

The book is specially designed to investigate what skills and strategies are required in writing and speaking modules that distinguish the IELTS proficiency levels. There are a number of factors like Word Stress, Intonation, Rhythm and Cohesive Devices, which is required on behalf of the IELTS candidate in order to determine their assessment over four band scales: Fluency, Grammatical Range and Accuracy, Lexical Resource and Pronunciation. But how to attain all these skills is still a matter of discussion. Without understanding these technical aspects of English language, it is difficult for the IELTS candidate to score better in IELTS Speaking Test as this is the criteria for their oral proficiency. In non-native English country like India and China, no preference is given to learn all these skills. Only few study materials are provided to them to memorise the answers. No preference is to be laid in building of Rhetoric among the candidate. The major objective of the book is:

- ✯ Making the IELTS candidate proficient in speaking test by teaching them all the Rhetorical devices like *Word Stress, Intonation, Rhythm, Cohesive Devices, Fluency, Lexical Resource*, etc.
- ✯ All these techniques should be properly designed and provided to the students in the form of study materials.
- ✯ Sound recorder (self-created by students in mobile phones) software should be used to maintain the Rate of Speech in the IELTS Speaking Task 2
- ✯ Speech therapies should be given to the students to twist their tongues in L2.

In 2001, the IELTS interview format and criteria were revised. A major change was the shift from a single global scale to a set of four analytical scales focussing on different aspects of oral proficiency. This study is concerned with the validity of the analytical rating scales. It aims to verify the descriptors used to define the score points on the scales by providing empirical evidence for the criteria in terms of their overall focus, and their ability to distinguish the levels of performance.

The Speaking Test Band descriptors and the criteria key indicators were analysed in order to identify the relevant analytic categories for each of the four band scales: *fluency*, *grammatical range* and *accuracy, lexical resource* and *pronunciation*.

Speaking Skills Checklist is as follows:

Production Skills, Pronunciation: Rhythm, Number & Length of Pauses, Stress, Intonation, Contours.

Communication Skills: Fluency, Clarity, Coherence, Confidence, Cultural Appropriateness, etc.

Language Skills: Grammatical Accuracy, Grammatical Range, Vocabulary

But how an IELTS student will build these skills is still the matter of discussion. The IELTS Books/Instructors or even the organization of IELTS are silent in this matter. No doubt, we can get this matter by netsurfing over different websites but what about the authenticity of the study material. The main problem in a non –native English country like India is that how students twist their tongues in L2 (English language) because while learning, they automatically get the influence of L1 (Mother Tongue) because it is their native language, and this is natural, so nobody can avoid it. But learning global (English) language with the help of Vocal Cosmetics/Rhetorical Devices will improve their tongue twisting into L2 (Second Language Acquisition) which automatically improve the proficiency of the candidate in the IELTS Speaking and Writing Test.

Keeping this viewpoint in mind, I have decided to put forth some technical aspects of learning, writing and speaking English through the medium of this book.This will truly help the students to speak good and perfect English.

ABSTRACT

This chapter contains the 'W' family of Vocal Cosmetics, i.e., What is Vocal Cosmetics? Why is it necessary to know Vocal Cosmetics? How can you learn Vocal Cosmetics? What are its ingredients, etc. This whole chapter makes the students aware how the technical part of English is important along with its grammar part.

Chapter 1 : 'W' Family of Vocal Cosmetics

1. What is Vocal Cosmetics?

Vocal cosmetics is the technical product for improving your voice or pronunication to enhance the second language.

2. Why Do We Need Vocal Cosmetics for IELTS?

The nine bands of Speaking Test depend only upon the ingredients of Vocal Cosmetics. This book will help you to know what are those factors that contribute a lot in building up of Speaking Bands. Speaking English is not just enough for scoring good bands in the Speaking Test, rather it requires candidate must be adept in the art of speaking English .

The basic problem with the candidates during Speaking TEST are as follows:

1. **No idea of the subject:-** Generally, it has been seen that most of the candidates don't have matter to speak on the topics given by the instructor.

   Solution in VOCAL COSMETICS :- This book helps the candidate to enhance the power of vocabulary with the tools of AWARENESS SESSIONS & LEXICAL RESOURCE.

2. **Problem of VOICE FUMBLING :-** Most of candidates face fumbleness in speaking the second language and many of them have their voice interrupted by their respective mother tongue as their mother tongue are their native languages.

   Solution in VOCAL COSMETICS :- This book will help the candidate with the techniques of SPEECH THERAPY.

3. **GRAMMATICAL ERRORS :-** The common problem with every candidate is lack of grammatical skills which require proper understanding of tenses, content and functional words.

   Solution in VOCAL COSMETICS :- This book will help in the building the structure of tenses with the help of the FINGER's GAME.

4. **TECHNICAL ENGLISH :-** Some important techniques are required to score the higher bands in the SPEAKING TEST like WORD STRESS, INTONATION, RHYTHM, SYLLABLE, COHERENCE .Vocal cosmetics is the answer of all these techniques with illustrations.

3. What are the ingredients of Vocal Cosmetics?

The main ingredients of Vocal Cometics are:

1. WORDSTRESS – 1BAND
2. INTONATION – 1 BAND
3. RHYTHM – 1 BAND
4. PAUSES – 1 BAND (PART OF SPEECH THERAPY)
5. FLUENCY – 1 BAND (PART OF SPEECH THERAPY)
6. COHERENCE – 1 BAND
7. GRAMMAR ACCURACY – 1 BAND
8. SECOND LANGUAGE ACQUISITION (L2) – 1 BAND
9. LEXICAL RESOURCE (VOCABULARY USAGE) – 1 BAND

4. How can it be Implemented?

With the help of *Speech Therapy Techniques,* it can be implemented.

ABSTRACT

This chapter provides the 'W' family of Interview Session. What is required for a good interview session with the instructor. Along with this, it also teaches us the Do's and Don'ts related to IELTS.

Chapter 2 : Interview Skills

Q 1. What is an Interview?

Ans. A view of inner personality, virtues caliber and expertise on the behalf of an individual.

2. Know "WH" Family

Who? What? Where? When? How? Why?

3. Interview Skills

Self-Awareness, Body Language, Communication, Intellect, Knowledge and Attitude to Understand the Query.

4. Do's for an Interview

- Give Extended Responses
- Be Concise and to the point
- Be Grammatically Correct
- Speak in Simple Small Sentences
- Usage of Appropriate English Words
- Trouble-Shooting
- Speak in Nice and Pleasant Tone
- Use Synonyms

5. Don't's for an Interview

- Do not put up fake accents
- Don't try to memorize answers
- Avoid usage of regional or vernacular words
- Don't throw in big names and words

6. Appearance

- Uniform or Casual Wear
- Clean, tidy and comfortable
- Hair should be combed

7. Look - Lap – Listen

- Sit up straight
- Look up
- Hands on your lap
- Be happy, smile and be friendly

8. End of the Interview

- Look at the interviewer
- Thank you
- Goodbye
- Close the door behind you quietly

Chapter 3
ABSTRACT

This chapter contain the detailed description of ingredients of Vocal Cosmetics with illustration and its manner of using while speaking English. The main ingredients of this chapter includes WORD STRESS SYLLABLE, INTONATION, RHYTHM, FLUENCY AND COHERENCE.

WORD STRESS

The Art of Word Stress Management:

English is a stressed language. STRESS is the degree of force with which we pronounce a sound.

TIP NO. 1	TEETH TOUCHING
TIP No. 2	PITCHING OF VOICE
TIP No. 3	USE PAUSES/SPEAK LOUDLY
TIP No. 4	STRESS ON VOWELS

Illustration for Word Stress Management:

1. John is leaving Paris **next week**. (Emphasize the time)
2. John is leaving **Paris** next week. (Emphasize the place)
3. John is **leaving** Paris next week. (Emphasize the action)
4. John **is** leaving to Paris next week. (Emphasize the truth)
5. **John** is leaving to Paris next week. (Emphasize the person)

SYLLABLE

A syllable is a unit of pronunciation uttered without interruption, loosely, a single sound. All words are made from at least one syllable.

- *Monosyllables* have only one vowel sound;
- *Polysyllables* have more than one vowel sound.
- If a syllable ends with a consonant, it is called a *closed syllable*.
- If a syllable ends with a vowel, it is called an *open syllable*.
- Patterns of syllables can be shown with C and V (C for ‘consonant’, V for ‘vowel’)
- Closed syllables are shown as CVC
- Open syllables CV

There are many words in English that have only one syllable.

- Cat
- House
- The
- Like
- Run

There are many more words that have two or more syllables.

- River (2 Ri-ver; CV-CVC)
- Doctor (2 Doc-tor; CVC-CVC)
- Happy (2 Hap-py; CVC-CV)
- Computer (3 Com-pu-ter; CVC-CV-CVC)
- Beautiful (3 Beau-ti-ful; CV-CV-CVC)

Pronunciation (5 Pro-nun-ci-a-tion; CV-CVC-CV-V-CVC)

INTONATION

Intonation is the variation of the pitch of the voice. Sometimes, the pitch of our voice rises, sometimes it falls and at other times, it remains at a certain level.

TIP NO.1	High Pitch at the beginning of a sentence
TIP No. 2	Low Pitch at the end of a sentence
TIP No 3	Important Notes with high pitch
TIP No.4	Maintain Gestures

For Instance –

Go and Open The Window

- When this statement is spoken with a RISING TONE, it becomes an order.
- When FALLING TONE is used for it , it becomes a request.The same case happens with the usage of polite words, such as please and thank you. Your usage of the tone will either make your listener pleased /angry.

FALLING TONE	RISING TONE
Ordinary Statements	Incomplete Sentences
Ordinary Commands	YES/NO Answers
Ordinary exclamations, polite requests	

Question Tags: - when the speaker expects the listener to agree with her	Repetition questions
Rhetorical Questions	Expected Questions
	Alternative Questions
	Enumeration

Rising tones in after: Thought, doubt, hesitation, greetings, parties, apologies and encouragement.

RHYTHM & FLUENCY

As you know, spoken English words with two or more syllables have different stress and length patterns. Some syllables are stressed more than others and some syllables are pronounced longer than others.

The same is true of *phrases and sentences*. Different words in a sentence have stronger stress and are pronounced longer and other words are weaker and shorter. *This pattern of strong and weak stress and short and long pronunciations gives English its rhythm.*

It is important for non-native speakers to understand and master the rhythm of English. If the wrong words are stressed in a sentence, or if all words are pronounced with the same length or loudness, the speech will be difficult to understand.

Content Words

Words that have the most stress in English are called the *content words*. Content words are usually the *nouns, verbs, adjectives, adverbs* and *pronouns (demonstrative, possessive, reflexive, and interrogative)*. These words are important to express the main meaning of the sentence.

Nouns: Terry, car, dinner
Verbs: Eat, study, drive
Adjectives: Blue, large, oval
Adverbs: Quietly, smoothly, equally
Pronouns: That, their, himself, what

Function Words

Function words are those words that are *weaker and shorter*. They include *auxiliary verbs, prepositions, conjunctions, determiners* and *possessive adjectives*. These words are less important in expressing the meaning of the sentence.

Auxiliary verbs: may, do, have (if not the main verb)

Prepositions: under, around, near

Conjunctions: but, not

Determiners: the, some, each

Possessive adjectives: my, your, our

COHERENCE

When sentences, ideas, and details fit together clearly, readers can follow along easily, and the writing is coherent. The ideas tie together smoothly and clearly. To establish the links that readers need, you can use the methods listed here. Note that good writers use a combination of these methods. Do not rely on and overuse any single method – especially *transitional words*.

1. Repetition of a Key Term or Phrase

This helps to focus your ideas and to keep your reader on track.

Example:

The problem with contemporary art is that it is not easily understood by most people. Contemporary art is deliberately abstract, and that means it leaves the viewer wondering what he he/she is looking at.

2. Synonyms

Synonyms are words that have essentially the same meaning, and they provide some variety in your word choices, helping the reader to stay focussed on the idea being discussed.

Example:

Myths narrate sacred histories and explain sacred origins. These traditional narratives are, in short, a set of beliefs that are a real force in the lives of the people who tell them.

3. Pronouns

This, that, these, those, he, she, it, they and we are useful *pronouns* for referring back to something previously mentioned. Be sure, however, that what you are referring to is clear.

Example:

When scientific experiments do not work out as expected, they are often considered failures until some other scientist tries them again. Those that work out better the second time are the ones that promise the most rewards.

4. Transitional Words

There are many words in English that cue our readers to relationships between sentences, joining sentences together. See below for a table of transitional words. There you'll find lists of words, such as however, therefore, in addition to, also, but, moreover, etc.

Example:

I like autumn, and yet autumn is a sad time of the year, too. The leaves turn bright shades of red and the weather is mild, but I can't help thinking ahead to the winter and the ice storms that will surely blow through here. In addition, that will be the season of chapped faces, too many layers of clothes to put on, and days when I'll have to shovel heaps of snow from my car's windshield.

Note that transitional words have meaning and are not just used at the beginnings of sentences. They can also be used to show relationships between different parts of the same sentence. As mentioned above they cue readers to relationships between sentences/clauses. If you use the wrong transitional word, then you confuse your reader. It would be better if you didn't use any transitional word rather than the wrong one. Furthermore, you do not need a transitional word at the beginning of each sentence. Good writers rarely use them as they achieve coherence by using other techniques. Many students overuse transitional words. Your instructor will guide you as to what problems you may have with transitions.

5. Sentence Patterns

Sometimes, repeated or parallel sentence patterns can help the reader follow along and keep ideas tied together.

Example: (from a speech by President John F. Kennedy)

"And so, my fellow Americans: ask not what your country can do for you--ask what you can do for your country."

Commonly Coherent Words

Addition		
again also and and then besides	equally further(more) in addition (to...) indeed next	in fact moreover too what is more finally
Comparison		

compared with in comparison with in the same way/manner	similarly likewise	again also
Contrast		
besides but however in contrast instead conversely it may be the case that certainly also likewise	naturally nevertheless of course on the contrary on the other hand regardless granted like different from alternatively	still whereas while yet although despite it is true that notwithstanding
Enumeration		
first(ly) secondly, etc. finally in the (first) place	last to (begin) with more important	on top of (that) next then
Concession		
although it is true that it may appear regardless certainly	granted that naturally it is true that I admit that	of course it may be the case that
Exemplification		
as (evidence of...) for example for instance thus to illustrate	such as to show what (I mean) specifically let us (take the case of...)	
Inference		
if not, ... in (that) case	otherwise that implies	then
Summary/Conclusion		

in all in brief to summarise in summary	in short in conclusion therefore In a nutshell	on the whole to sum up basically
Time and Sequence		
after (a while) afterwards at first at last at (the same time) while first , second, third... thereafter concurrently soon as soon as	before (that time) finally in the end meanwhile next immediately next firstly , secondly, thirdly... in the future subsequently at that time	since (then) so far then (up to) (then) later somewhat earlier shortly over the next (2 days) as long as last
Result		
accordingly as a result consequently since as a consequence of... caused accordingly	for that reason hence thus if...then... ...result(s) in ... contribute to in consequence	then therefore the (consequence) of that is... ...is due to... brought about by/ because... lead to...
Reformulation		
in other words rather briefly put simply	that is (to say) to put it more (simply) basically	
Replacement		
again alternatively	(better) still on the other hand	the alternative is...
Transition		

as far as ... is concerned as for ... incidentally	now to turn to... with (reference) to	with regard to... concerning...
Place/Position		
above beyond in the back nearby elsewhere opposite to behind	adjacent here near there far to the left	below in front there closer to farther on to the right
Miscellaneous - Adverbs may be used at the beginning of sentences to show how the sentence which follows relates to the rest of the text. Many of them reveal the writer's attitude to the idea they are expressing and so can be used as an important tool in evaluative writing.		
Admittedly All things considered As a general rule As far as we know Astonishingly Broadly By and large Characteristically Clearly Coincidentally Conveniently Curiously Disappointingly Equally Essentially Explicitly Even so Eventually Fortunately	Fundamentally Generally speaking Interestingly Ironically In essence In general In particular In practice In reality In retrospect/hindsight In theory In view of this More interestingly More seriously More specifically Naturally On balance Obviously On reflection Overall	Paradoxically Potentially Predictably Presumably Primarily Probably Remarkably Seemingly Significantly Surprisingly Theoretically To all intents and Purposes Typically Ultimately Understandably Undoubtedly Unfortunately With hindsight

ABSTRACT

This chapter awares the candidate how to use and improve the ingredients of Vocal Cosmetics in their speech with the help of therapies of speech. It awares above what is speech therapy, why it is necessary and how it is used as well as helpful for cracking the interview session of IELTS.

Chapter 4 : Speech Therapy

Target

Through this Vocal Cosmetic devices students will improve the rate of STAMMERING, FUMBLING AND PAUSES in their speech. This Therapy is an exercise for their *vocal cords* which includes *five skills*.

Technique

This device of Rhetoric will help the non-native English candidates to create the environment of English by their own. No doubt, recording will be the best way to improve the speech. But the candidates from the non-native English country need step-by-step learning and speaking techniques. The technique of recording is not sufficient. Generally, it has been seen even after learning the ingredients of Rhetorical Devices (Word Stress, Intonation, Rhythm, Vocabulary, Grammar Accuracy) their tongues face the influence of L1.

How is it Helpful?

This is natural but with the help of speech therapists and speech therapy techniques, candidates receive the filaments of L2 which will not allow them to face the hurdle of L1. This whole process is called as SECOND LANGUAGE ACQUISITION. (The second language Acquisition is a process by which people learn a second language in addition to their native language. The term, second language is used to describe the acquisition of any language after the acquisition of mother tongue). In simple terms, **IELTS-TECH focusses L1 (MOTHER TONGUE)to L2 (SECOND LANGUAGE ACQUUISITION)**

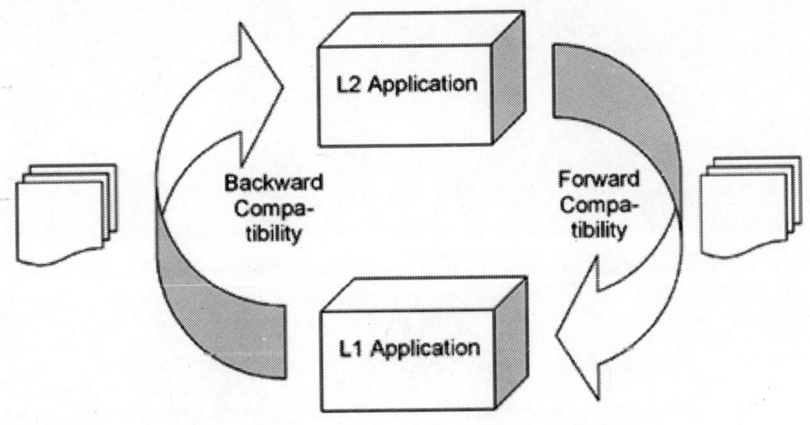

The four basic techniques of *Speech Therapy* which IELTS-TECH focusses on are:

1. **Reading Therapy:-** Allow the candidates to speak loudly in English Language with the help of ingredients of Rhetorical Devices (Word Stress, Intonation, Rhythm, Vocabulary, Grammar Accuracy)
2. **Grid Therapy:-** Allow the candidates to get the answers of the 'WH' family of Cue-cards and explain them on the spot. Allow the candidates to speak loudly in English Language with the help of ingredients of Rhetorical Devices(Word Stress, Intonation, Rhythm, Vocabulary, Grammar Accuracy)
3. **Listening Therapy & Conversational Therapy:-** "It is a common saying English is learn that from Ears. Allow the candidate to feel the lips, mouth and tongue twisting habits of Foreign Accents. Do share and converse with your friends the common questions related to your life as mentioned in CONVERSATIONAL THERAPY.
4. **Oral Therapy:-** Allow the candidates to speak from their brains with the help of the Art of the Imagination and the Art of using the "Wh" family, while producing the ideas and thoughts.

Strategy: To Build These Therapies

Record Your Voice in L2 (SECOND LANGUAGE – ENGLISH) in the following ways:-

1. Reading Therapy
2. Tongue Twisters
3. Grid Therapy
4. Conversational Therapy
5. Oral Therapy

READING THERAPY

TACT NO. 1 – HOW TO BUILD UP SKILLS FOR READING THERAPY

Time Duration:- 1 hr daily

- Using Word Stress Accent & Syllable (Described earlier)
- Speak Loudly
- Maintain Your Intonation & Rhythm (Described earlier)

Tips For Practising:

- READ & SPEAK AT LEAST 3 times by using WORD STRESS & SYLLABLES
- RECORD YOUR VOICE AND NOTICE THE CHANGE

PRACTICE EXERCISE - 1

Flo/wer/s are the swee/test things God ever made and for/got to put a soul into them. They are the soul of nat/ure. People be/lieve that earth la/ughs thro/ugh flo/wer. Flo/wers add beauty and co/lou/r to the surroundings. I love flo/wer but my fav/ou/rite flo/wer is rose. It is also known a 'king of flo/wers'. It is fam/ous for its exo/tic fra/gra/nce. It is found in different col/ou/rs. Red rose is the symbol of love and cou/rage. Yellow rose is the sym/bol of fri/end/ship. Yellow rose with red tip sym/bo/lizes friend/ship fall/ing into love. Whi/te rose sym/bo/lizes pe/ace and pu/ rity. Fur/ther/more, this flower in/cul/cates the seeds of op/ti/mism du/ring tri/al and tri/bu/la/ tions. As this flo/wer is sur/round/ed by tho/rns, thus it tea/ches us that every cloud has a sil/ ver lin/ing. On diff/erent occa/sions, rose is used to ex/press the feel/ings. On Va/len/tines Day lovers give red rose to show their love and a/ffec/tion. Be/sides this, red rose was also the fav/ ou/rite flo/wer of Pan/dit Jawa/har Lal Nehru. He used to wear this on his coat. Red rose is con/ si/dered to be the choice of ar/isto/cratic peo/ple.

During weddings or any other fun/ctions, the de/co/ra/tion by di/ffer/ent flo/wers is gain/ ing mo/men/tum these days. Rose is gen/era/lly used by extra/va/gant and rich people for bea/uti/fi/ca/tion of their pa/lac/es and houses. Red rose plays a sig/ni/fi/cant role to moll/ ify the sen/ti/ments of our lo/ved ones. Rose pe/tals or flo/wers are also used to wor/ship God. So I can say that red rose is the most spe/cial gift best/owed to us by nat/ure. But I really feel gri/ef/ed by see/ing the bell/iger/ent act/ion of peo/ple to/war/ds such a nice gift of Al/migh/ty. Co/mmon man is pluck/ing the flo/wers un/necess/arily. The red rose or any other flo/wer blo/sso/m on/ly when they are at the/ir appro/pria/te places like fie/lds, trees and on bran/ches of plants etc. Vase, walls of house is not the real pla/ces of flowers. One must not sep/arate any spe/cie/s of flo/wer from their com/pan/ions other/wise like ti/ger/s are near to ex/tinc/tion, one day we will really miss the exi/sten/ce of flo/wers also.

To con/clude, I would like to say, flowers can make us smile, when they blo/sso/m. So protect them and pay your gra/ti/tude to nat/ure for gifting such a beau/ti/ful thing on earth.

PRACTICE EXERCISE -2

Television is a mass media. It is an important and cheapest source of entertainment. It also serves as a reservoir of information. People like to watch television in order to unwind after a long day. I am a busy bee. So I do not have much time to watch television. But, I remember in my last summer vacations I have watched a documentary on elections in one of the Indian state. There were a lot of irregularities in those elections and they were effectively highlighted. For once, it made me sit back and think what is going on in Indian politics. India is supposed to be biggest democratic country in the whole world. But this democracy is misused by some of our corrupted politicians and industrialists. When I saw this documentary, I was totally shocked. In the documentary, they showed the horrible side of our politicians and how they toss law as a 'beach ball'. Politicians are the public servants but now they are trying to be their Lord. It also highlighted that how weak is common man in our country? It really touched my heart and gave me motivation to be altruist.

The programme left a strong impression that I personally should do something to restore law and democracy in this country. So now, I am a proud member of a social club named as 'Proud to be Indian'. It is a small club in my society and our purpose is to aware the common man about their rights and duties. If I can put things in order even for very few people then I would say that the purpose of my life is fulfilled. I am so glad that such programmes are telecasted these days. There is so much openness and transparency. People are free to make such programmes and present their own point of view. The general public is also free to draw their own conclusions and form their own opinions. More and more programmes of this kind should be produced and shown to the general public.

In this way, practise one or two paragraphs everyday for one week and notice the change in your speech.

TONGUE TWISTERS

TACT NO. 2 – HOW TO BUILD UP SKILLS FOR TONGUE TWISTERS

Time Duration: - 1 hr daily

Tongue Twisters : It is a phrase or sentence which is hard to speak fast, usually because of alliteration or a sequence of nearly similar sounds. It helps in removing pasus and fumbling in the speech and make it more clear and lucid.

Tips For Practising:

- READ & SPEAK AT LEAST 3 times everyday for one week .The practice of these exercises removes the fumbling of words and allows the user the acquisition of SECOND LANGUAGE.
- RECORD YOUR VOICE AND NOTICE THE CHANGE

TONGUE TWISTER FOR PRACTICE SESSIONS

- I wish to wish the wish you wish to wish, but if you wish the wish the witch wishes, I won't wish the wish you wish to wish.
- Picky people pick Peter Pan Peanut-Butter, 'tis the peanut-butter picky people pick.
- If Stu chews shoes, should Stu choose the shoes he chews?
- If Pickford's packers packed a packet of crisps, would the packet of crisps that Pickford's packers packed survive for two and a half years?
- Mr. Tongue Twister tried to train his tongue to twist and turn, and twit an twat, to learn the letter "T".
- How many cookies could a good cook cook, if a good cook could cook cookies? A good cook could cook as much cookies as a good cook who could cook cookies.
- How much ground would a groundhog hog, if a groundhog could hog ground? A groundhog would hog all the ground he could hog, if a groundhog could hog ground.
- Thirty-three thirsty, thundering thoroughbreds thumped Mr. Thurber on Thursday.
- How many berries could a bare berry carry, if a bare berry could carry berries?
- Well, they can't carry berries (which could make you very wary) but a bare berry carried is more scary!
- The great Greek grape growers grow great Greek grapes.
- Rory the warrior and Roger the worrier were reared wrongly in a rural brewery.
- Five fat friars frying flat fish.
- Shy Shelly says she shall sew sheets.
- I thought a thought.But the thought I thought wasn't the thought I thought I thought. If the thought I thought I thought had been the thought I thought, I wouldn't have thought so much.
- Once a fellow met a fellow in a field of beans. Said a fellow to a fellow, "If a fellow asks a fellow, Can a fellow tell a fellow What a fellow means?"

- Bill had a billboard, Bill also had a board bill. The billboard bored Bill so Bill sold the billboard to pay for the board bill.
- I feel a feel a funny feel a funny feel feel I, If I feel a funny feel a funny feel feel I.
- Dick had a dog, the dog dug, the dog dug deep, how deep did Dick's dog dig? Dick had a duck, the duck dived, the duck dived deep, how deep did Dick's duck dive? Dick's duck dived as deep as Dick's dog dug!
- A wooden worm wouldn't be worthy of worship but would he if he wondered and worried about what he would be worthy of if he wasn't wooden?
- There was a writer called Wright, he taught his son to write Wright right: "It's not right to write Wright 'Rite', please try to write Wright right!"
- Betty Better bought some butter, but she said, "this butter's bitter! But a bit of better butter will but make my butter better." So she bought some better butter, better than the bitter butter, and it made her butter better so 'twas better Betty Better bought a bit of better butter!
- I thought a thought. But the thought I thought wasn't the thought I thought I thought. If the thought I thought I thought had been the thought I thought, I wouldn't have thought so much.
- Peter Piper picked a peck of pickled peppers, if Peter Piper picked a peck of pickled peppers, whereas, the peck of pickled peppers Peter Piper picked?

GRID THERAPY

TACT NO. 3 – HOW TO BUILD UP SKILLS FOR GRID THERAPY?

Time Duration: - 1 hr daily

Solved Examples

Cue-Card 1

TALK ABOUT YOUR FAVOURITE CHILDHOOD TOY

- What that toy was?
- Who and when was it given to you?
  Where is it now?

HOW TO ANSWER A QUESTION [Make Notes]

- Introduction related to concept (childhood), then step by step come to the question, i.e., toy
- What : Name of the toy- A remote controlled car, (explain its features; colour, operating system and qualities)
- Who, When : Grandfather on my sixth birthday.
- Where : Talk about how well you have preserved it. If not, then WHY?

(Now Speak)

Well, childhood is the most precious stage of a man's life because one does not have any worries or tensions, children love to play with different kinds of toys. Even I used to play with lots of toys but my favourite toy was a remote controlled car gifted by my grandfather on my sixth birthday.

FEATURES OF CAR

- Red in colour, remote operated, chargeable battery
- Take turns, musical horns, move forward and backward lights
- Movable seats, skids, high speed and range of remote, breaks, dickey and doors open

" W" FAMILY

- Would play after coming back from school
- Forget to study, get scolding from parents

CONCLUSION

- No doubt, have I am grown up now, still its with me, placed nicely in my Almirah.
- My grandfather is no more, token of love, great remembrance.

Cue-Card 2

DESCRIBE YOUR FAVOURITE MOVIE

You should say:

- Which is the movie?
- Why has the movie impressed you so much?
- You can give your own suggestions.
- Explain how it influences you.

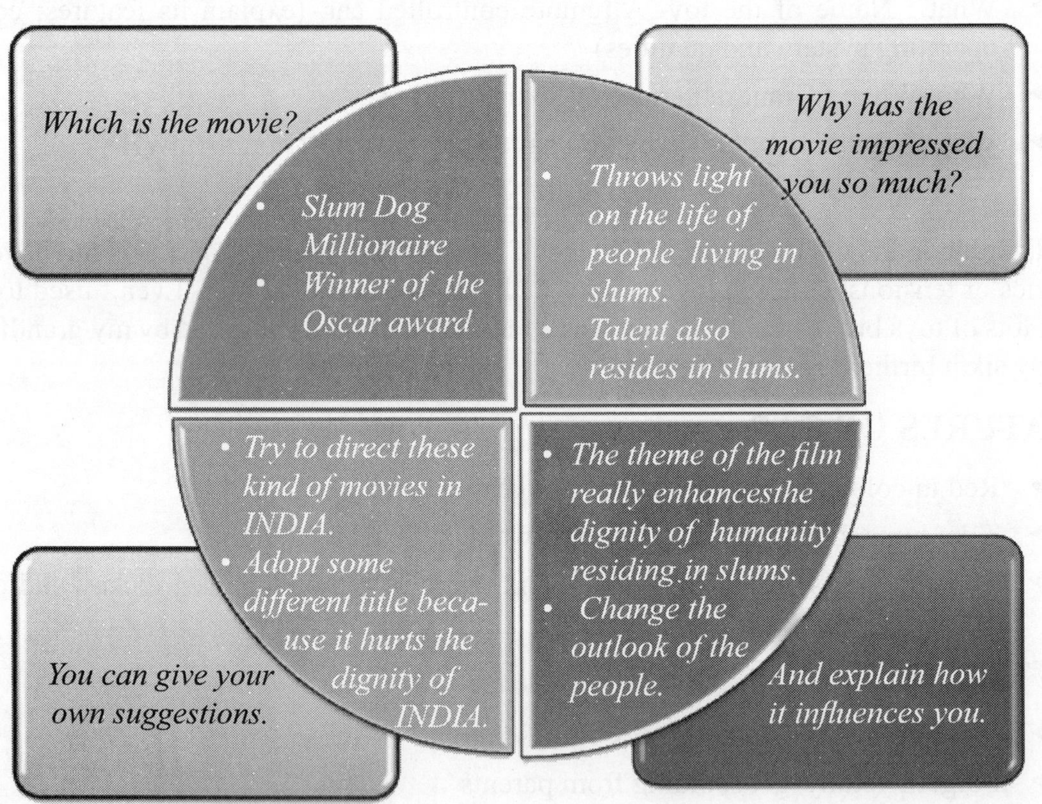

(Make notes on paper like this)

Cue-Card 3

DESCRIBE YOUR FAVOURITE GADGET

You should say:

- Which is the gadget?
- Why do you like that gadget?
- How it does help you?
- Explain whether it brings change in to your life.

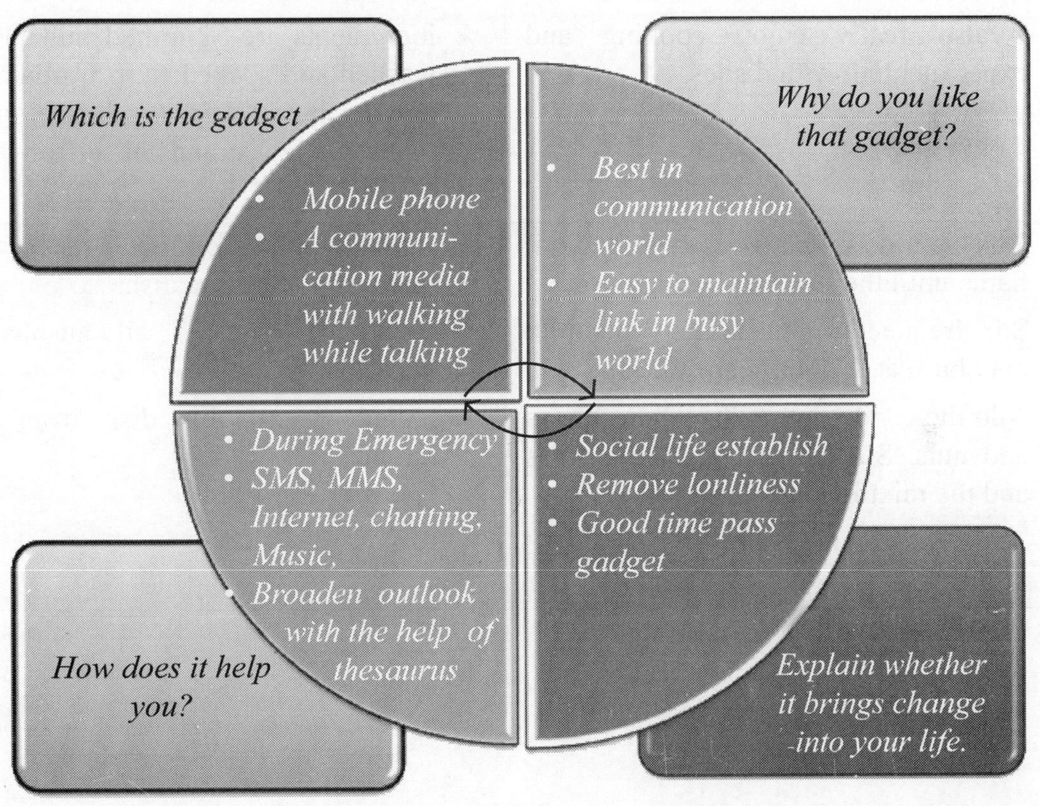

(Make notes on paper like this)

Cue-Card – 4

Talk about a Traditional Dish.

- Name of the dish.
- How is it prepared?
- Why is this your favourite dish.
- From where you come across this dish?

★ Fond of eating ★ Love to relish my taste buds with new and unique dishes ★ I also really enjoy cooking and experimenting with dishes.	★ Rice pudding is my favourite traditional dessert. ★ also known as *kheer*. ★ ingredients are Skimmed milk, Rice washed and soaked,1 tsp Cardamum powder, nuts, raisins (optional), sugar to taste, a few strands of saffron
★ Boil the rice in the milk on a medium flame until the rice is cooked. ★ Stir frequently; otherwise your milk may burn at the bottom of the vessel. ★ Add the condensed milk, sugar, raisins and nuts. Stir till the sugar dissolves and the mixture thickens. ★ Add the cardamom and serve hot.	★ I have a sweet tooth and that's why this is my favourite dish. ★ It is the soul of all auspicious occasions. ★ I have learnt this dish from my mother.

Cue-Card 5

DESCRIBE ANY NATIONAL DAY

You should say:

- ▶ Which is the day?
- ▶ Why is it celebrated?
- ▶ How is it celebrated?
- ▶ Explain what do you do on this day?

World Aids Day

✯ World AIDS Day ✯ Celebrated on 1st December	To prevent the masses from this dreadful epidemic ✯ To console those who are already addicted to it
UNAIDS Organization creates awareness by holding documentary consultations through media ✯ On individual grounds serves humanity by giving them recognition ✯ Telecasts its pros and cons	Donate something to the AIDS Organizations Hold Seminars to highlight this problem

Cue-Card 6

DESCRIBE A WELL-KNOWN PERSON YOU LIKE OR ADMIRE.
You should say:

- Who is this person?
- What has this person done?
- Why this person is well-known
- Explain why you admire this person?

INTRODUCTION:- Every person has his favourites and has his reasons that why he likes any famous personality. Some people are liked for their looks, brains, sports, qualities or for any other reasons.

MAHATMA GANDHI

Father of the nation. No longer alive but things taught are relevant today. Bapu, Great soul, Born on 2nd october, also celebrated a National Holiday and the International Day of Non-violence.	Britishers were ruling India. Weak and frail man could not impress much people but strong ideas, gave us twin concept of **Ahimsa** and **Swaraj** which became the slogans of India`s struggle for freedom.
Spent a number of years in jail, did not believe in violence, believed in passive resistance, Path he taught was not easy to follow but a sure shot way to success, millions of Indians were his followers, On 30 the January, 1948, Gandhi was shot while he was walking to a platform from which he was to address a prayer meeting. Still alive in our hearts, even today movies are made to highlight his ideology.	Campaigns to ease poverty, expand women's rights, build religious and ethnic amity, end untouchability, and increase economic self-reliance. Dandi march protest against the British-imposed salt tax, launched the *Quit India Civil Disobedience Movement in 1942,* **demanding immediate independence for India.**

Cue-Card 7

DESCRIBE A SONG OR A PIECE OF MUSIC YOU LIKE
You should say:

- What the song or music is?
- What kind of song or music it is?
- Where did you first heard it?
- Explain why do you like it?

INTRODUCTION :- Music is the wine that fills the cup of silence. It is a food for the soul. It is the best source of entertainment. It rejuvenates our mind and body. It has a universal language which is not bounded by regions or religions. It ignites a spark of love even in the heartless soul.

FOLK MUSIC

Punjabi folk music is highly rhythmic and very diverse. The contemporary Punjabi music is not just enriched by mixing up new tunes and beats of western music of today own but it is extremely enriched by its origin.	Though, new dimensions have been added to the folk Punjabi music, in order to make Punjabi music an International music. Punjabi people are very hard working and posscssivc, Punjabi music artist and singers do hard work and researches on music.
Basic roots and instruments of the Punjabi folk music are the same as those of Rajasthan, Gujarat, Haryana and other parts of North-western India, but the Punjabi, music retains a certain beat and rhythm which is unique to it. It is also influenced by the neighbouring country, i.e., Pakistan.	Traditional Punjabi songs were forgotten for some years when the pop style music arrived suddenly, but now the pop fever is over and artists and people are returning back to their traditional music. Types of Punjabi folk music are sufi, ghazals, classical, quawali, etc. Singers- Bally Sagoo, Daler Mehndi, Mika, Harbhajan Mann etc., gave recognition to the Punjabi music in Bollywood. Gurdas Mann, Jaspinder Narula, Jazzy B, Jassi, Sartaj (Ghazal), Hard Kaur, Hans raj Hans (sufi), and many more.

Cue-Card 8

DESCRIBE ONE OF YOUR FRIEND

You should say:

- How did you meet him/her?
- How long you have known each other?
- How do you spend time together?
- Explain why you like this person.

INTRODUCTION :- Friendship is a sheltering tree. It's a unique blend of affection, loyalty, love, respect, trust and loads of fun. True friendship is perhaps the only relation that survives in the trials and tribulations of time and remains unconditional.

The friend I admire most is DAISY

Childhood friend Met in 7th standard At that time shifted to new school. Only one who liked me. Always their in my trials and tribulations. Stalwart and laborious too. Down to earth True friend. Still best friends No scope of show off. Hardly meet but still in touch via emails.	As we cannot survive without fresh air similarly cannot survive without true friends. Can talk to her everything with a surety that they will never be leaked to a third person. Sit and vent out all my feelings. Listen to me patiently and suggest me a solution.
Always there to improve me. My worst critic but constructive one. Did a number of small silly things together but also the topper in class.	Silent bond. Deep bonding. Kind-hearted, altruist, versatile,

Cue-Card 9

DESCRIBE A FESTIVAL THAT IS IMPORTANT IN YOUR COUNTRY
You should say that:

- When does the festival occur?
- What you did during it?
- What you like or dislike about it?
- Explain why this festival is important.

INTRODUCTION :- Festivals act like vehicles that carry our culture, religion and history to a new generation. It breaks the monotony of a hectic and engrossed life. It provides an opportunity to meet friends and relatives. It helps to make a strong social bond.

DIWALI

Also known as Deepawali Festival of lights Comes in the month of October or November Related to the Hindu and Sikh history Feasts and festivals are a feature of all major religions	After the exile of 14 years, Lord Rama came back to his kingdom Ayodhya Deity of sikh community set himself free along with 52 kings from the prison in Gwalior
Helps to attract tourists and foreign investors. Plays a great role in the economy of India. Government can add special features by offering special discounts on tariffs during the festive season. Solemnise these festivals with great zeal and enthusiasm as they break the barriers of religion, class and region.	Celebrated with great pomp and show Brings people together Worship Goddess saraswati Lightening with candles and divas Fireworks are the main attraction Golden Temple`s Diwali is worldwide famous

Cue-Card 10

DESCRIBE AN INTERSTING HISTORICAL PLACE
You should say:

- What is it?
- Where is it located?
- What should you see there?
- Why is this place interesting or historical?

Introduction:- India is blessed with a number of world heritage monuments showcasing the breathtaking architecture and intricate work. Five thousand years of Indian History has given us the treasure of thousands of monuments across the country, monuments belonging to the Hindus, Buddhists, Muslims and Christians. Behind each monument, is an underlying sense of mystery, story, intrigue and romance.

A unique masterpiece, wonder in itself, an absolute epitome of Indian Culture, heritage and civilization. Agra, India situated on the bank of river Yamuna. Built in 1632-1653 by Ustad Ahmad Lahauri as architect, in the mughal architectural style, and about twenty thousand workers were recruited across Northern India to complete this wonderful piece of architecture.	Most recognizable structures in the world, built by Mughal Emperor Shah Jahan in memory of his third wife, Mumtaz Mahal. One of the most beautiful buildings in the world and stands as a symbol of eternal love. Finest example of the mughal architecture, a style that combines elements from Persian, Islamic and Indian architectural styles.
Marble glows with different colours depending on the time of the day, the graceful spires, domes and arches that seem to be the work of super human force with otherworldly talents, Indian architects call it as the 'LOVER' 'PARADISE'. Recent threats have come from environmental pollution on the banks of the Yamuna river including a ACID RAINS due to the Mathura Oil Refinery.	The bodies of Mumtaz and Shah Jahan were put in a relatively plain crypt beneath the inner chamber with their faces turned right and towards Mecca. The Taj Mahal was constructed using materials from all over India and Asia and over 1000 elephants were used to transport the building materials.

TACT NO. 4 – CONVERSATIONAL THERAPY

- Describe your hometown?
- What are you doing these days?
- What do you do when you have a holiday?
- What kind of music do you enjoy most?
- Do you have a hobby?
- Why have you chosen as your hobby?
- What kind of food do you like?
- Who is your best friend?
- Do you like shopping?
- What is your favourite colour?
- What are your strengths?
- What are your weaknesses?
- Describe your family?
- Who is your best friend?

TACT NO. 5 – ORAL THERAPY

This therapy is a combination of the above mentioned therapies. We utilize all the four tacts i.e. READING, TWISTING, GRIDING & CONVERSATIONAL Therapy.

TIPS

Step 1 :- Introduce the topic

Step 2 :- Discuss "the answers of the "W Family"

Step 3:- Use Rhetorical devices (Introduction, Meaning, Causes, Effects, Solutions and Conclusion) i.e., wordstress, intonation, rhythm, fluency, coherence and lexical resource.

Step 4 :- Conclusion of the topic.

ABSTRACT

The Interview Session Part (3) Speaking Test always require an introduction of the candidate. Under this section students are observed from the view points of etiquettes, exposure and efficiency so that to become more active in the interview session. It is necessary the introduction should be very comprehensive and meaningful.

Chapter 5 : Art of Introduction

1. Stand up straight.
   If you're sitting, stand up to shake hands. Don't hunch or lean over.
2. Extend your right hand.
   Keep a distance of roughly an arm's length when extending your hand to the other person. Stepping in too close could make her uncomfortable.
3. Grip the other person's hand firmly and gently shake.
   You always hear about the importance of firm handshakes, so it's shocking to get the dead fish. But, it happens quite often. Grip the other person's hand firmly, but don't squeeze. Practise with your own hands or with a friend to get a feel of your strength.
4. Use your first and last names.
   Instead of saying, "Hi, I'm Jane." Say, "Hi, I'm Jane Smith." This is a common young professional mistake. You should always use your first and last name in an introduction.
5. If they've already said their names, repeat it.
   "Peter, it's so nice to meet you. I'm Jane Smith."
6. If you introduce yourself first and then he introduces himself, repeat his/her name and say
   something nice.
   "Peter, it's a pleasure to meet you."
7. If you meet a lot of people, or are a public figure, you may want to avoid saying, "It's nice to meet you."
   Instead say, "It's good to see you." That way, if you've already met them and don't remember, you won't offend them. And, there's no harm in saying, "It's good to see you." It sounds just as pleasant and inviting.
8. Consider including your business.
   Depending on where you're at and your purpose, you may need to include the name of your organization in your introduction. For example, if you're at a conference introducing yourself with your company makes sense. "Peter, it's so nice to meet you. I'm Jane Smith from the ABC Company."
9. Consider including your title.

Including your title is a matter of personal preference, but is a good idea in many situations, especially as you climb the ranks. "Peter, it's so good to see you. I'm Jane Smith, the CEO at the ABC Company."

10. Consider including your relationship.

    "Peter, it's so nice to meet you. I'm Jane Smith. I'll be your Accounts Executive on this project."

    Or, "Peter, it's so nice to meet you. I'm Jane Smith from the ABC. I believe we have a mutual acquaintance.

    "Do you know Jim Baker from there?" This is an excellent way to start a conversation.

YOUR INTRODUCTION INCLUDES

- Name and Designation
- Personal Details
- Like Date of Birth, Age, Marital Status, etc.
- Educational Qualification
- Hobbies/Skills/Talents/Adjectives
- SWOT

SWOT

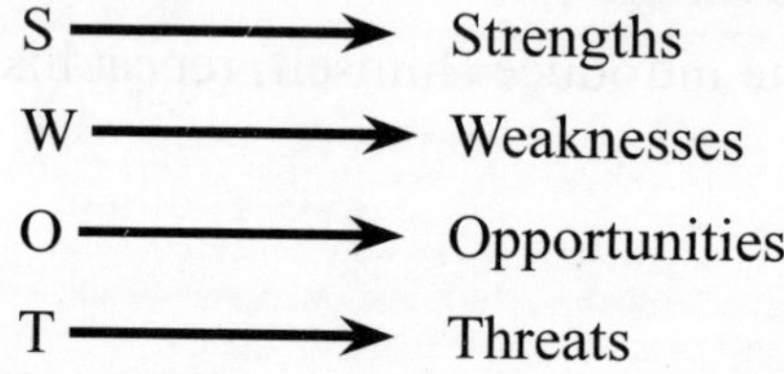

ABSTRACT

This chapter enhances the grammatical skills of the candidate which include the introduction note in sentences and tenses because while speaking during an interview session mistakes in tenses are quite common among the candidates. To enhance the skills of grammar and vocabulary, the Palm Game of Tenses is provided for a quick review of the candidates.

Subject VERB OBJECT

S V O

FOR SENTENCE CONSTRUCTION

- ✯ NOUN + PRONOUN = SUBJECT

  NOUN: Name or Place of description
- ✯ PRONOUN: Pronoun is the substitute of a noun

I st Person: I, My, Me, We, Our, Us

2nd person: You ,Your, Yours

3rd Person: He, She It, They, Their, Them, Him, Her, His, Name

V…..Verb of ENGLISH

Verb involves the action of the subject

O...... Object in English

S V9 O

RAM IS PLAYING FOOTBALL.

An object tells about subject

English Completes in FIVE Types of Sentences.

- ✯ Assertive Sentences
- ✯ Interrogative Sentences
- ✯ Imperative Sentences
- ✯ Exclamatory sentences
- ✯ Negative Sentences

WHAT ARE ASSERTIVE SENTENCES?

An assertive sentence is a simple sentence.

S V O

Sita Sings A Song

WHAT ARE INTERROGATIVE SENTENCES?

An Interrogative Sentence involves questioning in sentences.

V S O

Does Sita Sing A Song?

WHAT ARE NEGATIVE SENTENCES

A Negative Sentence involves "not" in sentences.

S N V O

Sita Does Not Sing A Song.

WHAT ARE IMPERATIVE SENTENCES

An Imperative Sentence is one which involves request, or command or an advice. Imperative Words are:

Please……May…….Order…….Suggestion………Pardon…….Forgive……Wishes……

Examples

Open the Door.

Please Give Me a Glass of Water.

May I come in !

WHAT ARE EXCLAMATORY SENTENCES?

An Exclamatory Sentence Involves Some Shocking and Surprising Aspect.

Exclamatory Words	S V O
Hurray !	We Won the match.

Alas! O! Goodbye! Forbade! Sorry! Wonder! Wow!

TENSES

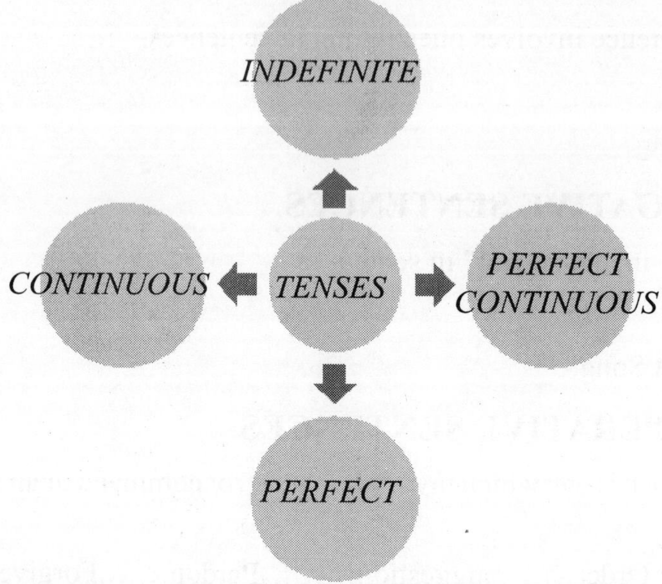

INDEFINITE

INDEX FINGER

PRESENT INDEFINITE

SUBJECT(S) VERB(V1) OBJECT(O)

PAST INDEFINITE

SUBJECT(S) VERB(V2) OBJECT(O)

FUTURE INDEFINITE

SUBJECT(S) Will/Shall VERB(V1) OBJECT(O)

CONTINUOUS

MIDDLE FINGER

PRESENT CONTINUOUS

SUBJECT(S) + Is/Am/Are + VERB(V1) + ing OBJECT(O)

PAST CONTINUOUS

SUBJECT(S) + Was/Were + VERB(V1) + ing OBJECT(O)

FUTURE CONTINUOUS

SUBJECT(S) + Will/Shall be + VERB(V1) + ing OBJECT(O)

PERFECT

RING FINGER

PRESENT PERFECT

SUBJECT(S) Has/have + VERB (V3) + OBJECT(O)

PAST PERFECT

SUBJECT(S) + Had + VERB (V3) + OBJECT(O)

FUTURE PERFECT

SUBJECT(S) + Will have /Shall have + VERB (V3) + OBJECT(O)

PERFECT CONTINUOUS

SMALL FINGER

PRESENT PERFECT CONTINUOUS

SUBJECT(S) + Has/have been + VERB (V1) + ing + Since/for + OBJECT(O)

PAST PERFECT CONTINUOUS

SUBJECT(S) + Had been + VERB (V1) + ing + Since/for + OBJECT(O)

FUTURE PERFECT CONTINUOUS

SUBJECT(S) + will have/shall have been + VERB (V1) + ing + Since/for + OBJECT(O)

ABSTRACT

This chapter is a complete package of Vocabulary Usage for the IELTS candidates which includes as Volley of Idioms and Phrases that allows the candidates to make their English language more expressive with words. It also includes Synonyms and Antonyms for the awareness of the candidates which help them a lot in Reading, Writing and Speaking sections of the IELTS. Not only this, it includes the Vocabulary of Foreign Words and One – Word Substitutions in this whole package.

Chapter 7 : Lexical Resource (Vocabulary Usage)

(A) IDIOMS

S.no.	IDIOMS	MEANING	USAGE
1	Apart from	1.Except for 2. in addition to	Apart from the ending, the movie was really good.
2	At a stretch	In continuity	I can work twelve hours at a stretch
3	Back up	Support	The workers backed up their leader.
4	Be in the good books	Have a good impression on	Brilliant students are always in good books of their teachers.
5	By hook or by crook	By any means , fair or foul	By hook or by crook, I want to be rich.
6	Butter up	Flatter with an intention	Many of the colleagues are buttering up the manager for promotion.
7	By leaps and bound	Very swiftly	Our company is making progress by leaps and bounds.
8	Carry weight	Have great influence	His opinion always carries weight.
9	Cat and dog life	Life of dispute	It is better to get separated than living a cat and dog life in a joint family.
10	Coin money	Make much money quickly	He is coining money through his export business.
11	Character assassination	Bring bad name to an important public man	Character assassination of the rivals is very common in politics.
12	Close one's eye	Ignore	Many old people close their eyes to family matters

13	Eleventh hour	Last moment	Some students prepare for the exams only at the eleventh hour.
14	End in smoke	Come to nothing	All his schemes ended in smoke.
15	Fan the flames	Increase panic or excitement	Many political leaders fan the flames during communal riots for their selfish motives.
16	From pillar to post	From place to place	Even qualified engineers and doctors are running from pillar to post.
17	Flora and fauna	Plant and animal life of a region	In geography, we read about the flora and fauna.
18	Get rid of	Be freed of	I want to get rid of my nail biting habit.
19	Give a free hand	Give freedom to work as one wishes	He was given a free hand in his job
20	Give a false color to	Misrepresent	The media gave a false colour to the whole incident.
21	Go hand in hand	Be closely connected	Population growth and unemployment go hand in hand .
22	Grease the palm	Bribe	Greasing the palm has become very common in many government offices now.
23	Have the upper hand	Have control	He has the upper hand in everything the company does.
24	Hustle and bustle	Busy and noisy activity	I cannot tolerate any hustle and bustle when I am studying.
25	In a nutshell	In few words , in brief	In a nutshell, the situation is quitc worsc.

26	In full swing	In great progress , using full efforts	We are preparing for the exam in full swing.
27	In hot water	In trouble	He displeased his boss and is in hot water now.
28	Jack of all trades	Multi skilled person	It is good to be jack of all trades these days .
29	Keep ones eye open	Be alert	Keep your eyes open, the robber is hiding somewhere here.
30	Kill time	Waste time	He has nothing to do; he is just killing time.
31.	Kill two birds with one stone	Secure two purposes at the same time	By accepting night duty, I killed two birds with one stone. Now, I can earn money and attend the college in daytime.
32	Kith and kin	Friends and relations	His kith and kin had come to the airport to receive him.
33	Knock down	Demolish	The building was knocked down as it was illegal.
34	Lick one's boots	Serve like a slave	Some employees lick boss' boots to get promotion.
35	Laughing stock	An object of fun	That fat girl is the laughing stock of the whole college.
36	Make hay while sunshine	Seize opportunities	In this competitive world, it is necessary to make hay while the sun shines or we will lag behind.
37	Make both ends meet	Live within one's income	The cost of living has increased so much that many people find it difficult to make both ends meet.
38	Next door	In the next house or room	My best friend lives next door to me.

39	On the contrary	Used to emphasize that the opposite of what is just stated is actually true	It was not a good decision; on the contrary, it was a mistake.
40	On the spur of the moment	At once , without deliberation	I cannot give you a definite reply on the spur of the moment
41	On the top of the world	Extremely happy	When I was selected for the job , I felt on the top of the world.
42	One's cup of tea	Field of one's skill	Getting admission in MBBS is not everybody's cup of tea
43	Out of order	Not working	Half of the machines in the factory are out of order.
44	Paint the town red	Enjoy in a showy manner	They painted the town in red when their son returned.
45	Part and parcel	An essential part	Music is a part and parcel of my life.
46	Pile up	Accumulate, heap up	We piled up all the newspapers in the room.
47	Play tricks	Cheat	You can't play tricks with me.
48	Play safe	Not to take any risk	Let's play safe and not go there without a map.
49	Pros and cons	Reasons or considerations for and against	Check pros and cons before proceeding further.
50	Put an end to	Stop	We must put an end to all the wrong practices.
51	Red letter day	Day that is pleasantly noteworthy or memorable	Marriage is a red letter day in everyone's life
52	Raw deal	Bad treatment	Old people often get a raw deal from the society.

53	Rake up	Recall unnecessary from the past	Why are you raking up the issue after so long?
54	Sail in the same boat	Be in the same condition	It is hard time for both of us; we are sailing in the same boat.
55	Sugar the pill	Use sweet words to convey harshness	Don't try to sugar the pill. We know you well.
56	Take a stand	Support a view firmly	You have to take a stand now and favour only one of us.
57	The order of the day	That which is current or common now usual happening	Corruption in government offices is the order of the day.
58	A bed of roses	Easy and pleasant situation	Life is not always a bed of roses.
59	A drop in ocean	Very insignificant	Our knowledge about the universe is only a drop in the ocean.
60	A hard nut to crack	A difficult problem to solve	Hacking is a hard nut to crack.
61	A piece of cake	A task that can easily be accomplished	Dieting is not a piece of cake.
62	ABC	Elementary principles of a subject	I do not even know the ABC of dancing.
63	Along with	In addition to, together with	My three other colleagues also got promotion along with me.
64	Behind bars	In prison	All the criminals should be behind bars.
65	Bear with	Tolerate patiently	You need to bear with the inconvenience for sometime.
66	Blue-collar job	Job involving manual work	Many students have to survive on blue-collar jobs abroad before they get a degree.

67	Born with a silver spoon in mouth	Born in wealth and luxury	It is difficult for people born with a silver spoon in mouth to face real hardships of life.
68	Bread and butter	One's livelihood	Poor people struggle really hard to earn their bread and butter.
69	Burn one's fingers	Get oneself into trouble	He burnt his fingers by interfering in his neighbour's matter.
70	Burning question / issue	A very important question / issue that must be dealt with	Drug abuse is a burning issue.
71	Cry for the moon	Wish for something impossible	World peace is the cry for the moon.
72	Come into play	Come into action	Dishonesty has come into play in business nowadays.
73	Come across	Meet or find by chance	I came across an old friend to the market.
74	Draw back	Go back from one's undertaking	He drew back from the election.
75	White-collar job	Office job	Every graduate wants to do a white-collar job.

(B) PHRASES

Back out — To withdraw from a promise, contract : I felt grieved when he backed out of his promise to help me.

Back up — To support; to sustain : He backed up his report with relevant statistics.

Bear upon — To be relevant to : This argument does not bear upon the subject under discussion.

Blow up — To explode : The mine blew up and all the labourers working inside were killed. — to reprimand or scold : If you continue to be negligent, the teacher will blow you up.

Break down — Of a car; a piece of machinery; to go wrong so that it will not function : The car broke down on our way to Mumbai.

— To collapse; to succumb to uncontrollable weeping : She broke down completely on hearing the news of her husband's death.

— To succumb to a nervous collapse through overwork or worry: He worked so hard that his health broke down near the examination.

Break off — To end; to discontinue; to desist : We had to break off our conversation when he arrived. She broke off in the middle of the story. She did not like his nature and broke off the engagement.

Break up — To disperse; to dissolve : The college will break up for the Puja holidays on 25th October. The meeting will break up after the President has addressed the audience.

Bring up — To rear : Those brought up in adversity are able to cope with life better.

Call forth — To provoke : The minister's views on the disinvestgment policy of the government called forth a good deal of bitter criticism.

Call out — To shout : I called out to him but he disappeared in the dark.

— to announce by calling or shouting : The Manager called out to the peon that he was being immediately fired.

Call upon — To order; to require : I was unfortunately called upon to give evidence against him.

Carry on — To continue : If you carry on working hard, your business will soon flourish.

— to manage : He carried on his business so well that he soon amassed a huge fortune.

Cast away — To throw aside : You must cast away all your apprehensions and accept the offer.

Catch up with — To overtake; to draw level : Last week, I had to stay late at the office to catch up with some pending files.

Come off — To take place : The prize distribution came off on Tuesday last.

— to turn out successful : His speeches at the conference always came off beautifully.

Cry down — To deprecate; to make little of : You must not unneccessarily cry down the conduct of others.

Cry out against — To complain loudly against : The opposition parties cried out against the fast pace of the globalisation of the Indian economy.

Cut out — Designed for : Your were cut out to be a lecturer in a college.

Drop in — To visit casually : On my way to the college, I dropped in at Mira's place.

Drop out — As the race progressed, many children dropped out.

Fall back — To recede; to retreat : On seeing the armed guards, the civilians fell back.

Fall down — From a higher position to a lower one : The branch gave way and he fell down into the canal.

Fall off — To withdraw; to drop off : Some of our subscribers have fallen off. Friends fall off in adversity.

Fall under — To come under : This colony does not fall under my jurisdiction.

Get along — To prosper; to progress; to proceed : Well, doctor, how is your patient getting along? It is simply impossible to get along with him.

Get on with — To live pleasantly together; to progress : How are you getting on with your studies?

Get into — To be involved in : It is easy to get into scandals but hard to come out unscathed.

Give in — To surrender; to yield : I gave into her repeated requests and accepted the offer.

Give over — Not to do any longer : It is time you gave over pretending that you have access to the Prime Minister.

Go after — To follow; to pursue : The policeman went after the thief but the latter managed to escape in the dark of the night.

Go down — To be accepted : The terrorist attack onWTC will go down in history as one of the worst acts of terrorism.

Go without — To remain without : he is so poor that sometimes he has to go without food.

Go by — To follow : I am sorry to disappoint you but we have to go by the rules.

— To elapse (used of time) : Months have gone by but I have not called upon him.

Hang about — To loiter near a place : Last evening, I say your friend hanging about your house.

Hang upon — To depend upon : The success of any venture hangs upon the seriousness with which it is undertaken.

Hold out — To endure; to refuse to yield : How long can you hold out against starvation?
— To continue : Sugar stocks are not likely to hold out very long.
— To offer : She held out her hand to the Prince.

Hold to — Abide by : Whatever resistance there might be, I will hold to my decision.

Keep off — To ward off : His stern looks keep off the flatterers.

— To maintain : They have been trying to keep up their standard of living though there has been a considerable decline in their income.

Keep up with — To keep pace with : You read too fast; I cannot keep up with you.

Knock out — To win by hitting the opponent insensible in a boxing bout : The challenger was knocked out in two minutes.

Lay By — To put away for future use : She has laid by five thousand rupees to celebrate her marriage anniversary.

Lay in — To store for future use : Anticipating scarcity of foodgrains, they laid in a good store of provisions.

Let down — To fail a friend : Won't I feel grieved if my own friends let me down?

Let into — To suffer to enter; to admit : Despite his pleadings, they did not let him into the meeting. I shall let no one into my secrets.

Let out — To lease on hire : In my immediate neighbourhood, there is a decent house to let out.

— To loosen : Let us let out the dog for a while.

Look about — To study one's surroundings : The thief looked about himself before entering the house.

Look for — To search for : The old woman was looking for her spectacles.

Look up — To search for and find : Please look up this word in the dictionary.

— To have an upward tendency (said of prices): The price of sugar is loking up these days.

Make off with — To run away with : The servant made off with the master's watch.

Makeover — To transfer : He has made over the building to his son.

Make up — To supply what is deficient : You must work hard during the Dussehra holidays and try to make up your deficiency in English.

— To invent or fabricate : She made up a story to get rid of the visitor.

— To reconcile : They have made up their quarrel and are now getting on quite well.

Pass away — To die : His sister passed away in the early hours of the morning.

Pass by — To disregard; to omit : He did not invite me to his birthday. It appears that he passed me by.

— To go alongside of : You passed by my house the day before yesterday.

Pick out — To select or choose : The teacher picked out the best student from the class.

Pick up — To recover or regain health after an illness: He has become so weak that he will take two months to pick up.

Play upon — (a musical instrument) : She played upon the harmonium and sang a melodious song.

— To take advantage of : The blackmailer played upon her love for her husband.

Pull down — To demolish; to destory : The old house was pulled down to create space for multi-storey flats.

Pull up — To take to task : The teacher was always pulling him up for his bad handwriting.

Put off — To postpone : We had to put off the wedding till the war was over.

— To lay aside : He put off his shoes before entering the temple.

— To turn one aside from a purpose or demand: I approached him for some help but he put me off with mere words.

Put into — To drag into : Don't put me into the argument.

Put out — To extinguish : It is time to put out the light and go to sleep.
— To perturb, to annoy : I was put out on hearing that I had incurred heavy losses in the recent business transactions.

Run away — To flee : The little girl took a necklace and ran away.

Run away with — To steal and depart with : The cashier ran away with twenty thousand rupees.

Run off — To break off from control : The dog broke the chain and ran off.

Run over — To drive over : The car ran over the pedestrian as he was crossing the road.

— To flow over : The tant is running over.

Run through — To squander or waste : It took him only a few months to run through all the money his father had left him.

— To read quickly : I will just run through this lesson and tell you what it is all about.

— To pierce : The needle ran through her finger when she was stitching her shirt.

See into — To attend to : You can set right the situation if you see to it at an early date.

Set in — To begin : As soon as rains set in, it beecomes pleasant.

Set up — To establish; to open a new business : He is soon going to set up as a financier.

Speak for — To recommend somebody or to urge somebody's claims: If you speak form to the Manager, I am sure he will look at my case favourably.

Speak on — To deliver a lecture on : This evening I am going to speak on the changing concepts of morality in various ages.

Stand off — To keep at a distance : Would you please stand off? I brook no interference in my way of work.

Strike for — To stop work for some reason : The labourers have struck for higher wages.

Take after — To resemble : The younger sister takes after the elder one.

Take for — To form an impression about somebody's identity : I was taken for a South Indian.

Take in — To deceive : She thinks her oily tongue can take everybody in.

Take to — To become addicted to : He took to gambling and drinking at a very early age.

— To form a liking for : Of late, she has taken to painting.

Tell against — To prove adverse to; to go against : I am sure these facts are going to tell against your case.

Throw about — To fling here and there : to leave in disorder : The child threw his books about and ran off to play.

Throw away — To lose through carelessness : You have thrown away a golden opportunity.

Turn against — To become hostile to : I shall not give up my principles even if the whole world turns against me.

SYNONYMS & ANTONYMS

(C) SYNONYMS

A

Abandon : Leave, forsake
Abridge : Shorten, curtail
Abundant : Plentiful
Accumulate : Collect, store
Adequate : Sufficient
Adversity : Misfortune
Aggravate : Heighten, intensify
Attack : Assault
Authentic : True
Awkward : Clumsy

B

Behaviour : Demeanour
Bias : Prejudice
Brutal : Savage, cruel
Brisk : Bright, lively

C

Callous : Hard, cruel
Calm : Quiet, tranquil
Casual : Uncertain
Category : Class
Cold : Frigid, indifferent, passionless
Compassion : Pity, sympathy
Concise : Short, brief
Condense : Compress, thicken
Conversant : Familiar
Crafty : Cunning, sly
Cruel : Fierce, tyrannical

D

Damage : Loss, harm, injury
Decorate : Adron, embellish
Deformity : Malformation, disfigurement

Denounce : Accuse, condemn
Diligent : Industrious, persevering
Divine : Godlike, heavenly

E

Earnest : Serious, solemn
Emergency : Exigency
Exceptional : Unusual, rare
Extravagant : Wasteful, prodigal, spendthrift

F

False : Untrue, spurious
Fascinate : Charm, enchant
Ferocious : Fierce, savage
Fraud : Deceit, trickery

G

Genuine : Real
Gigantic : Colossal, great
Guilt : Sin, crime

H

Haughty : Arrogant, proud
Hazardous : Dangerous, risky, perilous
Humility : Modesty, politeness

I

Illiterate : Unlearned, ignorant
Imperious : Authoritative, dictatorial
Impertinent : Impudent, insolent, shameless
Inanimate : Lifeless
Inexorable : Relentless, merciless
Irresolute : Undecided, wavering, vacillating

J

Jolly : Jovial, merry
Judicious : Discreet, prudent

K

Knavery : Fraud

L

Laborious : Industrious
Lament : Grieve, mourn
Lethargy : Sluggishness
Liberty : Freedom, independence
Loathe : Detest, abhor
Lucky : Fortunate

M

Magnificent : Splendid, grand
Marvellous : Wonderful
Meagre : Small
Mean : Low, abject
Mighty : Strong, powerful
Misery : Sorrow, distress

N

Nice : Pleasant, agreeable
Notable : Remarkable, memorable
Notorious : Infamous

O

Obliterate : Destory, efface
Obsolete : Antiquated
Opportune : Timely

P

Pensive : Thoughtful
Perennial : Permanent, perpetual
Persuade : Induce, urge
Plentiful : Abundant
Precarious : Risky, dangerous
Pretence : Pretext, excuse

Q

Quaint : Queer, odd, singular
Queer : Strange, odd
Questionable : Doubtful

R

Radiant : Bright, brilliant
Refined : Elegant
Rejoice : Delight
Relevant : Pertinent
Renown : Fame, reputation
Repudiate : Reject
Resistance : Opposition
Rigid : Stiff, unyielding
Ruinous : Destructive, injurious

S

Sacred : Holy, consecrated, pious
Satiate : Satisfy
Scanty : Slender, meagre
Sensual : Fleshly, carnal
Shapely : Graceful, elegant
Solitary : Single, lonely
Sombre : Gloomy, dark
Specimen : Sample, model
Splendid : Magnificent, grand
Spurious : False, imaginary
Stiff : Rigid, stern
Superficial : Shallow
Surplus : Excess

T

Talkative : Garrulous
Temperate : Moderate
Thankful : Grateful, obliged
Thin : Slim, slender
Thrive : Prosper, flourish
Tough : Hard, strong, difficult
Tragic : Sorrowful, distressing

U

Ugly : Repulsive
Urbane : Polite, courteous, suave
Urge : Press, incite

Useful : Advantageous

V

Vacillatge : Waver
Venerable : Respectable
Vigilance : Watchfulness
Voracious : Greedy
Vulgar : Coarse, crude

W

Wealthy : Rich
Wickedness : Evil
Wild : Savage
Wretched : Miserable, unfortunate
Wreck : Ruin, destory

Y

Yield : Surrender
Yielding : Submissive

Z

Zeal : Passion
Zenith : Top, summit
Zest : Enthusiasm

(D) <u>ANTONYMS</u>

<u>A</u>

Ability : Disability
Accept : Reject, refuse
Acquit : Convict
Affinity : Aversion
Ancient : Modern
Artificial : Natural
Attract : Repel
Awkward : Graceful

<u>B</u>

Barbarous : Civilized
Barren : Fertile
Base : Noble
Benevolent : Malevolent
Bold : Timid, cowardly
Brutal : Humane, kindly

<u>C</u>

Callous : Soft, tender
Care : Neglect
Censure : Praise, applaud
Chaste : Impure, unchaste
Cheap : Dear
Cheerful : Gloomy, depressed
Competent : Incompetent
Conceal : Reveal
Condense : Lengthen, expand
Confess : Deny
Create : Destory
Credit : Discredit, debit

<u>D</u>

Danger : Safety
Deep : Shallow

Delight : Displeasure, sorrow
Dense : Sparse
Despair : Hope
Diffident : Confident
Distant : Near

E

Early : Late
Elevation : Depression
Emancipate : Enslave
Energetic : Weak
Enthusiasm : Indifference
Equality : Inequality
Explicit : Implicit
Exterior : Interior
Extrinsic : Intrinsic

F

Fabulous : Actual, real
Failure : Success
Fickle : Constant
Fine : Coarse
Folly : Wisdom
Foreign : Native
Fautility : Utility

G

Gain : Loss
Genuine : False
Gloomy : Gay
Guilty : Innocent

H

Happiness : Sorrow, sadness
Help : Hinder
Honour : Dishonour, shame
Humane : Cruel
Hypocrisy : Sincerity

I

Imperative : Optional
Increase : Decrease
Inhale : Exhale
Interested : Disinterested
Interesting : Uniteresting

J

Joyful : Sad, depressed
Junior : Senior
Justice : Injustice

K

Kind : Cruel
Knowledge : Ignorance

L

Lack : Plenty
Legal : Illegal
Legible : Illegible
Liberty : Slavery
Light : Heavy
Loose : Tight
Love : Hate

M

Mad : Sane
Malice : Goodwill
Master : Servant
Meagre : Plentiful
Merit : Demerit
Mild : Harsh, stern
Morbid : Healthy
Motion : Rest

N

Natural : Artificial
Noble : Base, Ignoble

Normal : Abnormal
Notorious : Reputable

O

Obstinate : Yielding
Offensive : Pleasing, defensive
Optional : Compulsory
Oral : Written
Outward : Inward

P

Part (n) : Yielding
Part (v) : Join
Particular : General
Peace : War
Persuade : Dissuade
Pleasure : Pain
Polite : Impolite, rude
Praise : Condemn, defame
Precious : Cheap, worthless
Pride : Humility
Prudent : Imprudent
Punishment : Reward

Q

Quick : Slow, tardy

R

Raise : Lower
Rash : Steady, cautious
Rear : Front
Receive : Give
Reject : Accept, admit
Religious : Secular, irreligious
Remember : Forget
Rich : Poor, needy
Rise : Fall

S

Sacred : Unholy, profane
Satisfaction : Dissatisfaction
Scanty : Plentiful
Sensitive : Insensitive
Service : Disservice
Sharp : Blunt
Silence : Noise
Sober : Excited, drunk
Sophisticated : Naive
Special : Ordinary
Stale : Fresh
Straight : Crooked
Superior : Inferior
Surplus : Deficit
Swift : Slow

T

Tedious : Lively
Temperate : Intemperate
Thankful : Thankless
Thrifty : Extravagant
Timid : Bold
Tranquil : Agitated
True : False

U

Ugly : Beautiful
Union : Disunion, discord, split
Urban : Rural
Usual : Unusual

V

Vain : Modest
Violent : Gentle
Virtue : Vice
Vulgar : Refined.W

Wane : Wax
Want : Abundance
War : Peace
Wild : Civilised

<u>Y</u>

Yield : Resist

(E) FOREIGN WORDS AND PHRASES

1. Ab initio (Latin)	From the beginning
2. Aborigine (Latin)	Native, any of the earliest known inhabitants of a certain region
3. Actionnaire (French)	Shareholder
4. Actualite (French)	Real existence; appropriateness
5. Ad hoc (Latin)	For the special purpose
6. Ad interim (Latin)	In the meantime; temporary
7. Ad libitum (Latin)	As one pleases
8. Ad referendum (Latin)	For further consideration
9. Ad valorem (Latin)	According to value
10. A Dio (Italian)	To God; Addio!Adieu!
11. Agamemnon (Greek)	The leader of the Greeks in the Trojan war, king of Mycenae
12. Aide (French)	An assistant, a helper, a mate
13. Air noble (French)	An air of distinction
14. Ajax (Latin, Greek)	The Greek hero next to Achilles in the Trojan war
15. Alectryon (Greek)	A cock
16. Allah it Allah (Arabian)	There is no God but the God the Muslim war cry
17. Alopecia (Latin, Greek)	Fox mange : a skin disease, which destroys the hair; baldness

18. Allure (French)	Mien, gait, air
19. Alpeen (Irish)	A cudgel
20. Alter ego (Latin)	One's second self, a very close friend, a representative
21. Affair d'amour (French)	A love affair
22. A'la mode (French)	According to the custom; in fashion
23. Alma Mater (Latin)	Benign mother; A term applied by students to the school, college or university where they have been educated
24. Anno Christi (Latin)	In the year of Christ
25. Anno Dontini (Latin)	In the year of Christ
26. Ante Meridiem (Latin)	Before noon
27. Ars longa, vita brevis (Latin)	Art is long, life is short
28. Au contraire (Latin)	On the contrary
29. Au revoir (French)	Adieu, until we meet again
30. Auto (Spanish)	An act, a drama
31. Bacchus (Latin, Greek)	The god of wine
32. Basta (Italian)	Enough ! No more!
33. Bastide (French)	A French country house
34. Beau garcon (French)	A handsome man
35. Beau jour (French)	Fine day, good times

36. Beaux-arts (French)	The fine arts
37. Beneficiare (French)	The person receiving benefits
38. Bene qui latiut bene vixit (Latin)	He has lived\ell who has lived obscure
39. Billet-doux (French)	A love letter
40. Bonn fide (Latin)	In good faith
41. Bon hoinie (French)	Good nature
42. Bonjour (French)	Good day; good morning
43. Bon voyage (French)	A good journey to you
44. Boutique (French)	A shop. tradesman's stock
45. Bourgeoisee (French)	The social class between the aristocracy and the working class; middle class
46. Bravo (Italian)	Well done; splendid
47. Cadre (French)	A frame, a scheme; a list of officers
48. Cafe (French)	Coffee
49. Camaraderie (French)	Comrade; Friendly fellowship
50. Carpe diem (Latin)	Enjoy the present day
51. Cara sposa (Italian)	Dear wife
52. Chef (French)	A cook in charge of a kitchen; head cook
53. Chesara' Sara' (Italian)	What will be will be
54. Cognito, ergo sum (Latin)	I think, therefore, I am

55. Coiffeur (French)	Hair dresser
56. Contra (Latin)	Against
57. Corpus (Latin)	The body of a man or animal, especially a dead body
58. Coup d'etat (French)	Sudden decisive blow in politics
59. Creme (French)	Cream
60. Creme de la creme (French)	Cream of the cream; the very best
61. Danke, Schoon (German)	Many thanks
62. De bonne grace (French)	With good grace
63. De facto (Latin)	In fact, actually
64. De jure (Latin)	In the law; by right
65. Dei gratin (Latin)	By the grace of God
66. Deluxe (French)	Luxurious
67. Dennode (French)	Out of fashion
68. Desagrement (French)	Something disagreeable
69. Detenu (French)	A prisoner
70. Deus ex inachina (Latin)	A character or event brought artificially into the plot of a story or drama to settle an involved situation
71. Distrait (French)	Absent minded
72. Dramatis personae (Latin)	Characters in a drama or a play

73. Donna e' mobile (Italian)	Woman is changeable
74. Duce (Italian)	A leader
75. Ecce! (Latin)	Behold!
76. Edition deluxe (French)	A splendid and expensive edition of a book
77. Elegant (French)	A person of fashion
78. Elite (French)	The best part
79. En famille (French)	With one's family; at home; in an informal way
80. En masse (French)	In a group, universally
81. En prince (French)	In princely style
82. En queue (French)	In a string or line
83. En rapport (French)	In agreement, in accord with
84. En route (French)	On the way
85. Entente (French)	An understanding; agreement
86. Entrepreneur (French)	A business man
87. En rills (French)	In town, 'not at home'
88. Espirit de corps (French)	Group spirit, sense of pride
89. Errare est liumaru in (Latin)	To err is human
90. Estancia (Spanish)	A mansion

91. Ethos (Greek)	Permanent character; in literature and art, chief characteristics of a work as affecting the ıntellectual and moral faculties, as opposed to pathos which appeals to the emotions.
92. Etoile (French)	Star
93. Et tu, Brute ! (Latin)	You too,Brutus! (Caesar's exclamation, when he saw his much loved Brutus amongst the murderers.)
94. Euge! (Latin, Greek)	Well done!
95. Eureka (Meureka) (Greek)	I have found it
96. Excelsior (Latin)	Higher; (erroneously) upwards.
97. Exceptio confirmat (probat)	The exception proves the rule. regular (Latin)
98. Ex officio (Latin)	By virtue of his office
99. Ex post facto (Latin)	After the deed is done; done or made after wards
100. Extra (Latin)	Beyond, outside the scope of
101. Fade (French)	To become less distinct
102. Fait accompli (French)	A thing already done
103. Fenome (French)	Woman, wife
104. Festa (Italian)	A festival
105. Flair (French)	Aptitude; a natural talent or ability

106. Gallant (French)	Gay, elegant, attentive to ladies
107. Gens de letters (French)	Literaryman
108. Grand (French)	Great
109. Heil (German)	Flail!
110. Homo sapiens (Latin)	Mankind; human beings. III. Hotel (French) A hotel, a mansion
112. Id est (Latin)	That is
113. Ibidem (Latin)	In the same place, thing or case
114. In camera (Latin)	In the chamber of the judge
115. In toto (Latin)	In the whole; entirely
116. Impasse (French)	A deadlock
117. In memoriam (Latin)	In the memory of
118. In petto (Italian)	Secretly, not revealed
119. Inter alia (Latin)	Among other things
120. Inter alios (Latin)	Among the persons
121. Kinder (German)	Children
122. L'allegro (Italian)	The cheerful man
123. Libra (Latin)	A pound; a unit of weight
124. Lingua franca (Italian)	Mixed language
125. Litterateur (French)	A man of letters

126. Locus Standi (Latin)	A right to interfere
127. Magnum opus (Latin)	A great work
128. Malentendu (French)	Misunderstood; poorly conceived
129. Matinee (French)	Reception or entertainment held in the afternoon
130. Milieu (French)	Surroundings; environment
131. Modus (Latin)	Manner, mode
132. Modus operandi (Latin)	Manner of working
133. Monsieur (French)	Sir, Mr.
134. Monstre scare (French)	A popular public figure who is considered above criticism
135. Mon and (French)	My friend
136. Nil (Latin)	Nothing
137. Non (Latin)	Not
138. Octroi (French)	Duties paid at the gate of a city
139. Oninia vincist labor (Latin)	Labour overcomes all things
140. Opera (Latin)	Plural of opus. Musical works of a composer numbered in order of composition or publication
141. Oil (French)	Yes
142. Par excellence (French)	Eminently, beyond comparison

143. Par example (Latin)	For example
144. Persona grata (Latin)	A person who is acceptable or welcome
145. Postmortem (Latin)	Happening done or made after death
146. Post (Latin)	After, e.g., afternoon
147. Pater (Latin)	Father.
148. Potage (French)	Soup
149. Prima facie (Latin)	On first view
150. Quantum (Latin)	Quantity, or amount
151. Quasi (Latin)	As if, seemingly
152. Regime (French)	Form of government
153. Resume (French)	An abstract or summary
154. R.S.V.P. (Reponds si'l vous plait) (French)	Reply, if you please, an answer will oblige.
155. Suns souci (French)	Without care
156. Sine die (Latin)	Without a day being appointed
157. Status quo (Latin)	Existing affairs of state
158. Status quoante (Latin)	The state of affairs existing prior to a given event
159. Terra incognita (Latin)	An unknown country
160. Tete-a-tete (French)	A private or intimate conversation between two people
161. Ultra vires (Latin)	Beyond one's powers

162. Viamedia (Latin)	A middle course
163. Vice versa (Latin)	The order or relation being reversed, conversely
164. Vis-a-vis (French)	Opposite; face to face
165. Viva voce (Latin)	By word of mouth; orally
166. Vive la (French)	Long live!

(F) ONE-WORD SUBSTITUTION

A person who is out to destroy all government and order	Anarchist
Government by the people	Democracy
The whole mass of air surrounding the earth	Atmosphere
One who is not sure of the existence of God	Agnostic
A medicine which prevents infection by killing germs	Antiseptic
One who does something not professionally but for pleasure	Amateur
A statement open to more than one interpretation	Ambiguous
One who makes an official examination of accounts	Auditor
Marrying more than one wife or more than one husband at a time	Polygamy
The science that studies plants	Botany
The science which studies natural processes of living things	Biology
People working together in the same office or department	Colleagues
The state of remaining unmarried	Celibacy
The action of bringing into completion	Consummation
To give one's authority to another	Delegate
Study of the relation of living things to environment	Ecology
The action of looking within or into one's own mind	Introspection
One incapable of being tired	Indefatigable
A letter, poem, etc. whose auther is unknown	Anonymous
Work for which no salary is paid	Honorary

One who looks at the bright side of things	Optimist
One who cannot read or write	Illiterate
A game or battle in which neither party wins	Draw
Holding established opinions	Orthodox
Hater of women	Misogynist
The study of the origin and physical and cultural development of manking	Anthropology
The science which studies the crust of the earth	Geology
The science which studies animals	Zoology
Happening at one and the same time	Simultaneous
Murder or murderer of oneself	Suicide
Lasting only for a very short while	Temporary
Capable of being seen through	Transparent
The first speech delivered by a person	Maiden
The art practised by statesmen and ambassadors	Diplomacy
One who walks on foot	Pedestrian
One who lives on others	Parasite
One who speaks for others	Spokesperson
One who spends very little	Miser
One who prossesses several talents or gifts	Versatile
One who eats vegatables only	Vegetarian
A thing that is fit to be eaten	Edible
A statement absolutely clear	Explicit

A widespread disease affecting many people at the same time	Epidemic
A trade that is prohibited by law	Gala day
A desire that cannot be represed	Illicit
A method that cannot be imitated	Irrespressible
Remarks which do not really apply to the subject under discussion	Inimitable
A story that can hardly be believed	Incredible
A comparison that is out of place	Unmatchable
That which cannot be satisfied	Insatiable
A remedy which never fails	Infallible
A thing that cannot be seen with human eyes	Invisible
One who is very easily made angry	Irritable
An ordinary and common place remark	Platitude
A sum paid to a man for a piece of work	Remuneration
The act of violating the sanctity or destroying the property of a sacred place	Sacrilege
To make up one's mind and change it quickly	Vacillate
A person with a long experience of any occupation	Veteran
A place where clothes are kept	Wardrobe
A state of complete continence on the part of a woman	Virginity
A man who has too much enthusiasm for his own religion and hates other religions	Fanatic
One who makes calculations connected with insurance	Actuary
A country, etc. which is very distant	Remote

To send out of one's native country	Exile
A person chosen by parties who have a controversy to settle their differences	Mediator
Notice of death, especially in a newspaper	Obituary
Notice of death, especially in a newspaper	Obituary
Opinion contrary to accepted doctrines	Heresy
Great clapping and cheering	Applause
Exclusive possession of the trade in some commodity	Monopoly
Sole right to make and sell some invention	Patent

(G) PROVERBS

1. Absence makes the heart grow fonder.

When you are away from someone you love, you love them even more.

2. Accidents will happen.

Some unfortunate events must be accepted as inevitable.

3. Actions speak louder than words.

What a person actually does is more important that what they say they will do.

4. Advice is cheap.

It doesn't cost anything to offer advice.

5. Advice is least heeded when most needed.

When a problem is serious, people often do not follow the advice given.

6. Advisers run no risks.

It's easier to give advice than to act.

7. All cats are grey in the dark.

People are undistinguished until they have made a name.

8. All good things come to those who wait.

Patience brings rewards.

9. All that glitters is not gold.

Appearances can be deceptive.

10. All days are short to Industry and long to Idleness.

Time goes by slowly when you have nothing to do.

11. All is fair in love and war

Things that are done in love or war can often be excused.

12. All's well that ends well

There is a solution to everything even though there are doubts.

13. All that glitters is not gold.

What look good on the outside may not be so in reality.

14. All things grow with time - except grief.

As time goes by, grief subsides little by little.

15. All things are difficult before they are easy.

With practice things become easier.

16. All work and no play makes Jack a dull boy.

Everybody needs a certain amount of relaxation. It is not good to work all the time;

17. An apple a day keeps the doctor away.

Eating an apple every day can help to keep you healthy.

Other interpretation: A small preventive treatment wards off serious problems.

18. An empty purse frightens away friends.

When one's financial situation deteriorates, friends tend to disappear.

19. An Englishman's home is his castle.

An Englishman's home is a place where he feels safe, enjoys privacy and can do as he wishes.

20. An idle brain is the devil's workshop.

When you work you avoid temptation.

21. An onion a day keeps everyone away.

A humoristic version of "an apple a day..."

22. An ounce of prevention is worth a pound of cure.

It is easier to prevent something from happening than to repair the damage or cure the disease later.

23. Anger is the one thing made better by delay.

When you are angry, it is best not to speak or act immediately.

24. Any time means no time.

If the date of an event remains vague, it will never happen.

25. April showers bring May flowers.

Something bad or unpleasant today may bring good things in the future.

26. A bad tree does not yield good apples.

A bad parent does not raise good children.

27. A bad workman blames his tools.

Blaming the tools for bad workmanship is an excuse for lack of skill.

28. A bird in hand is worth two in a bush.

It's better to keep what you have than to risk losing it by searching for something better.

29. A broken friendship may be soldered but will never be sound.

Friendships can be rebuilt after a dispute but will never be as strong as before.

30. A burden of one's own choice is not felt.

Something difficult seems easier when it is done voluntarily.

31. A burnt child dreads the fire.

A bad experience will make people stay away from certain things.

32. A cat has nine lives.

1) Cats can survive many accidents because they land on their feet without injury.

2) Three lives = 3 years to play, 3 years to stray, 3 years to stay.

33. A chain is no stronger than its weakest link.

The strength of a group depends on each individual member.

34. A change is as good as a rest.

A change in routine is often as refreshing as a break or a holiday.

35. A dry March, a wet April and a cool May fill barn and cellar and bring much hay.

Harvest predictions according to the weather.

36. A fault confessed is half redressed.

Confession is the beginning of forgiveness.

37. A flower blooms more than once.

If you miss an occasion, you can avail of it at another time.

38. A fool and his money are soon (easily) parted.

A foolish person usually spends money carelessly.

39. A fool at forty is a fool forever.

If a person hasn't matured by the age of 40, they never will.

40. A friend in need is a friend indeed.

Someone who helps you when you are in trouble is a real friend

V&S OLYMPIAD GUIDE BOOK AND WORKBOOK SERIES (CLASSES 1-10)

ISBN : 9789357940504 ISBN : 9789357940511 ISBN : 9789357940528 ISBN : 9789357940535 ISBN : 9789357940542 ISBN : 9789357942447 ISBN : 9789357942454 ISBN : 9789357942461 ISBN : 9789357942478 ISBN : 97893579424

ISBN : 9789357940559 ISBN : 9789357940566 ISBN : 9789357940573 ISBN : 9789357940580 ISBN : 9789357940597 ISBN : 9789357942492 ISBN : 9789357942508 ISBN : 9789357942515 ISBN : 9789357942522 ISBN : 978935794253

ISBN : 9789357940405 ISBN : 9789357940412 ISBN : 9789357940429 ISBN : 9789357940436 ISBN : 9789357940443 ISBN : 9789357942546 ISBN : 9789357942553 ISBN : 9789357942560 ISBN : 9789357942577 ISBN : 978935794258

ISBN : 9789357940450 ISBN : 9789357940467 ISBN : 9789357940474 ISBN : 9789357940481 ISBN : 9789357940498 ISBN : 9789357942591 ISBN : 9789357942607 ISBN : 9789357942614 ISBN : 9789357942621 ISBN : 9789357942638

ISBN : 9789357942102 ISBN : 9789357940603 ISBN : 9789357940610 ISBN : 9789357940627 ISBN : 9789357940634 ISBN : 9789357942744 ISBN : 9789357942751 ISBN : 9789357942768 ISBN : 9789357942775 ISBN : 9789357942782

ISBN : 9789357940641 ISBN : 9789357940658 ISBN : 9789357940665 ISBN : 9789357940672 ISBN : 9789357940689 ISBN : 9789357942799 ISBN : 9789357942805 ISBN : 9789357942812 ISBN : 9789357942829 ISBN : 9789357942836

ISBN : 9789357940696 ISBN : 9789357940702 ISBN : 9789357940719 ISBN : 9789357940726 ISBN : 9789357940733 ISBN : 9789357942645 ISBN : 9789357942652 ISBN : 9789357942669 ISBN : 9789357942676 ISBN : 9789357942683

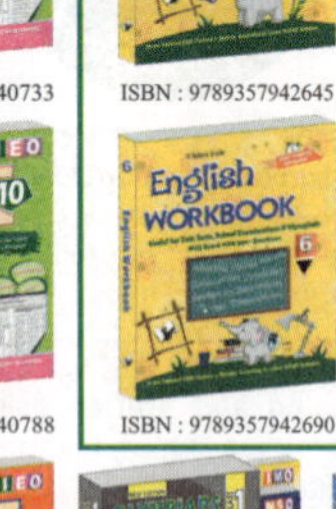

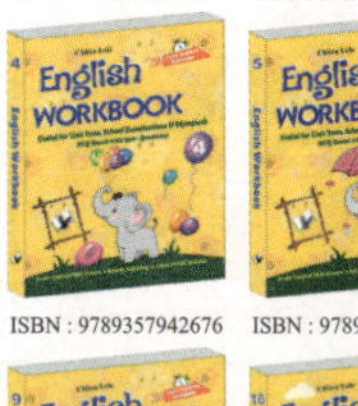

ISBN : 9789357940740 ISBN : 9789357940757 ISBN : 9789357940764 ISBN : 9789357940771 ISBN : 9789357940788 ISBN : 9789357942690 ISBN : 9789357942706 ISBN : 9789357942713 ISBN : 9789357942720 ISBN : 9789357942737

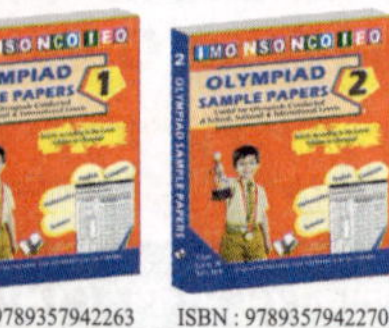

ISBN : 9789357942263 ISBN : 9789357942270 ISBN : 9789357942287 ISBN : 9789357942294 ISBN : 9789357942300 ISBN : 9789357942003 ISBN : 9789357942010 ISBN : 9789357942027 ISBN : 9789357942034 ISBN : 9789357942041

ISBN : 9789357942317 ISBN : 9789357942324 ISBN : 9789357942331 ISBN : 9789357942348 ISBN : 9789357942355 ISBN : 9789357942058 ISBN : 9789357942065 ISBN : 9789357942072 ISBN : 9789357942089 ISBN : 9789357942096

CAREER & BUSINESS/SELF-HELP/PERSONALITY DEVELOPMENT/STRESS MANAGEMENT

   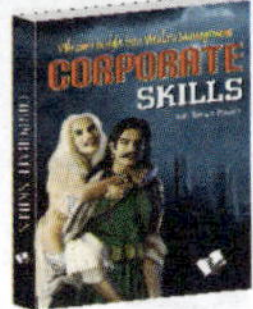   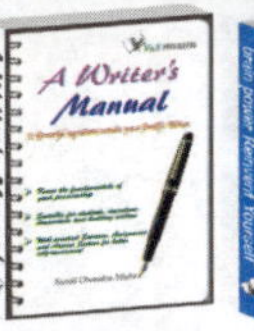 

ISBN : 9789381588789 ISBN : 9789350571637 ISBN : 9789381588512 ISBN : 9789381588963 ISBN : 9789381588598 ISBN : 9789381384039 ISBN : 9788192079622 ISBN : 9789350570753 ISBN : 9789381384396

ISBN : 9789381384541 ISBN : 9789350570968 ISBN : 9789381384527 ISBN : 9789381588666 ISBN : 9789381384541 ISBN : 9789381384107 ISBN : 9789350571187 ISBN : 9789381588574 ISBN : 9789381588277

       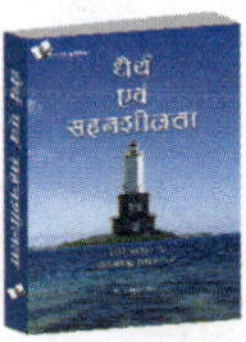 

ISBN : 9789381588222 ISBN : 9789381384213 ISBN : 9789381588772 ISBN : 9789381588949 ISBN : 9789357940108 ISBN : 9789381384152 ISBN : 9789381384145 ISBN : 9789381448564 ISBN : 9789381384473

 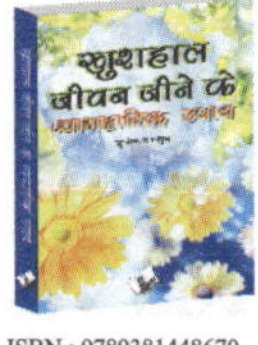  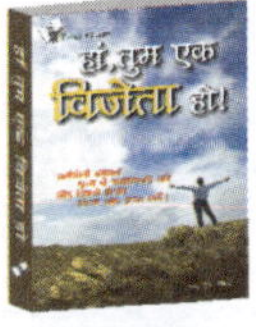    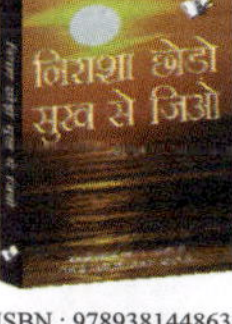

ISBN : 9789381448595 ISBN : 9789381448670 ISBN : 9789381588253 ISBN : 9789381448755 ISBN : 9789381448649 ISBN : 9789381384480 ISBN : 9789350571309 ISBN : 9789381448632 ISBN : 9789381384893

ISBN : 9789381384091 ISBN : 9789381384176 ISBN : 9789350570265 ISBN : 9789381588727 ISBN : 9789350570128 ISBN : 9789381588246 ISBN : 9789381448687 ISBN : 9789381448786 ISBN : 9789381448533

ISBN : 9789381448526 ISBN : 9789381384206 ISBN : 9788122310689 ISBN : 9789381384503 ISBN : 9789381588505 ISBN : 9789381448717 ISBN : 9788192079646 ISBN : 9789350570203 ISBN : 9789350570272

ISBN : 9789381588741 ISBN : 9789350571170 ISBN : 9789381588215 ISBN : 9789381384763 ISBN : 9789350570296 ISBN : 9789381588284 ISBN : 9789381588543 ISBN : 9789350571880 ISBN : 9789381588765

ISBN : 9789350570579 ISBN : 9789350571927 ISBN : 9789350571545 ISBN : 9789381384114 ISBN : 9789381384435 ISBN : 9789381448779 ISBN : 9789381448991 ISBN : 9789381384510 ISBN : 9789381384169 ISBN : 9789350570623

ISBN : 9789381448908 ISBN : 9789381448915 ISBN : 9789381448922 ISBN : 9789381448939 ISBN : 9789381448946 ISBN : 9789357940795 ISBN : 9789357940801 ISBN : 9789357940818 ISBN : 9789357941303 ISBN : 9789357941853

STUDENT LEARNING/QUIZ/POPULAR SCIENCE/BIOGRAPHIES

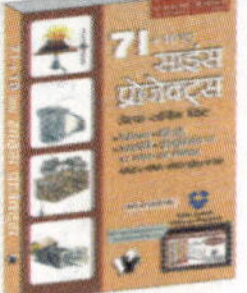

ISBN : 9789357941310
ISBN : 9789357941495
ISBN : 9789381384053
ISBN : 9789381384060
ISBN : 9789381384121
ISBN : 9788122310924
ISBN : 9789381588468
ISBN : 9789381588604
ISBN : 9789350570494

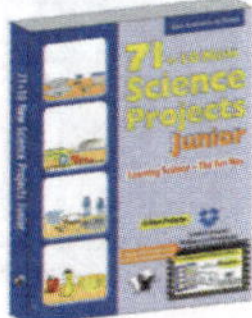

ISBN : 9789350570470
ISBN : 9789350570487
ISBN : 9789350570500
ISBN : 9789350570586
ISBN : 9789350571248
ISBN : 9789350571248
ISBN : 9789350571743
ISBN : 9789381384299
ISBN : 9789381448052

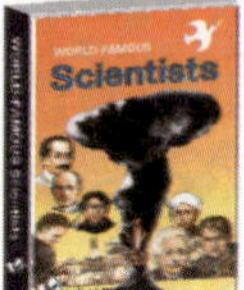

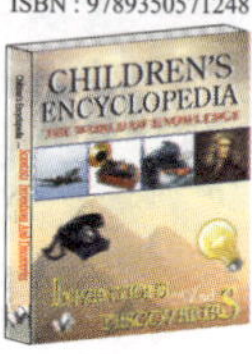

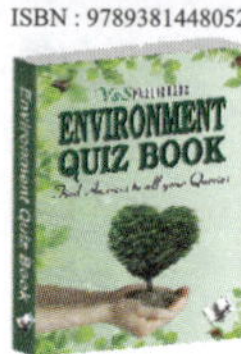

ISBN : 9789381384305
ISBN : 9789381384954
ISBN : 9789381588819
ISBN : 9789350570371
ISBN : 9789350570388
ISBN : 9789350570395
ISBN : 9789350570401
ISBN : 9789350570364
ISBN : 9789381588444

ISBN : 9789381448977
ISBN : 9789381384459
ISBN : 9789381384930
ISBN : 9789350571682
ISBN : 9789381588864
ISBN : 9789381588673
ISBN : 9789350570111
ISBN : 9789381384312
ISBN : 9789381588680

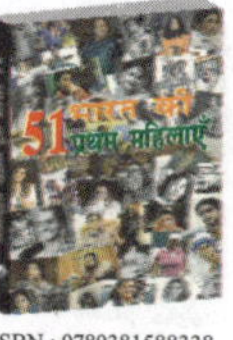

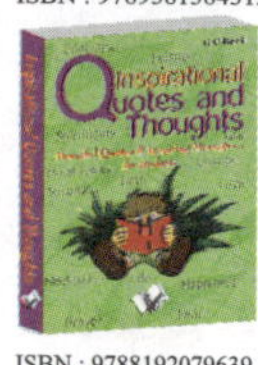

ISBN : 9789350570258
ISBN : 9789350570227
ISBN : 9789381588499
ISBN : 9789381588338
ISBN : 9789381588345
ISBN : 9789381448656
ISBN : 9789381384558
ISBN : 9788192079639
ISBN : 9789350571019

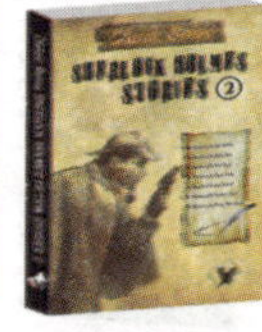

ISBN : 9789350571026
ISBN : 9789350571033
ISBN : 9789350571040
ISBN : 9789350571057
ISBN : 9789350570999
ISBN : 9789350571002
ISBN : 9789350571064
ISBN : 9789350571071
ISBN : 9789350571088

ISBN : 9789350571101
ISBN : 9789381588321
ISBN : 9789381588307
ISBN : 9789381588567
ISBN : 9789350571163
ISBN : 9789350570517
ISBN : 9789381384183
ISBN : 9789381448625
ISBN : 9789381384794

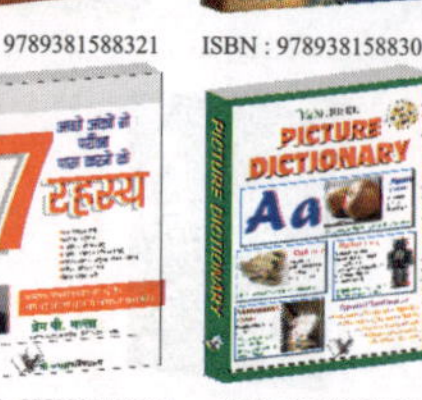

ISBN : 9789381384190
ISBN : 9789381448793
ISBN : 9789381588192
ISBN : 9789381588802
ISBN : 9789381588970
ISBN : 9789350570777
ISBN : 9789381448427
ISBN : 9789350570555
ISBN : 9789350570548

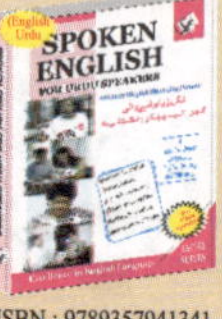
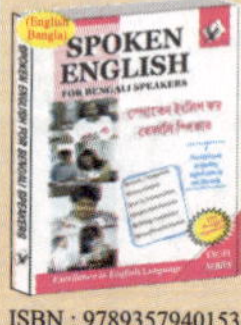
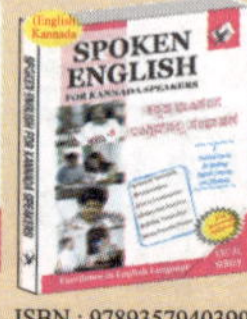
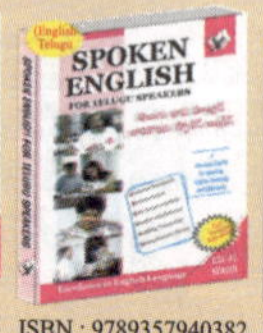
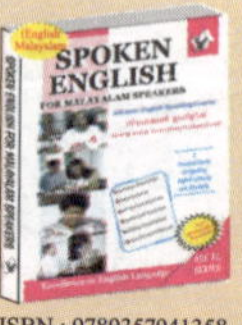
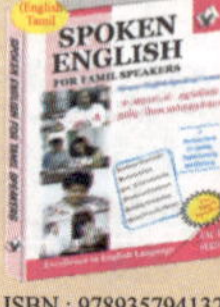

ISBN : 9789357940856
ISBN : 9789357940849
ISBN : 9789357941334
ISBN : 9789357941341
ISBN : 9789357940153
ISBN : 9789357940399
ISBN : 9789357940375
ISBN : 9789357940382
ISBN : 9789357941358
ISBN : 9789357941327

FICTION/FUN & FACT, TALES & STORIES/LEISURE READING

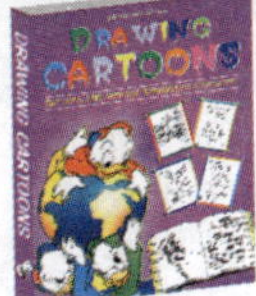

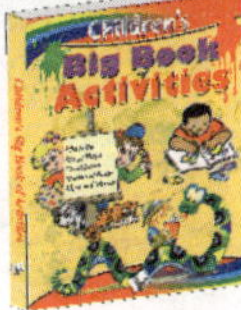

ISBN : 9788192079660 ISBN : 9788192079677 ISBN : 9789381588659 ISBN : 9789381588840 ISBN : 9789381588857 ISBN : 9789381588871 ISBN : 9789381588888 ISBN : 9789381384336 ISBN : 9789381448069

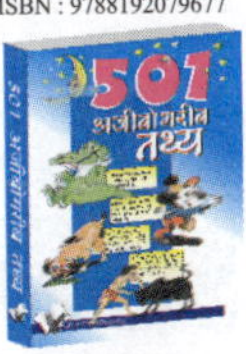
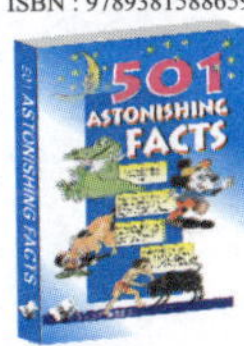

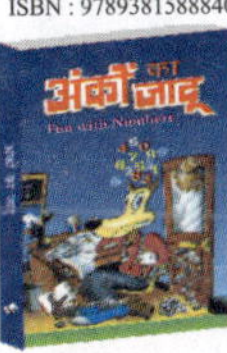

ISBN : 9789381448090 ISBN : 9789381448083 ISBN : 9789381384343 ISBN : 9789381448076 ISBN : 9789381448809 ISBN : 9789381448885 ISBN : 9789350571248 ISBN : 9789350570210 ISBN : 9789381384329

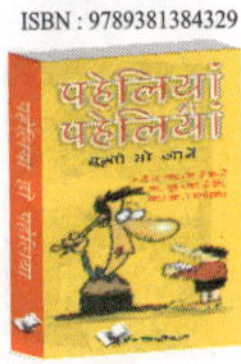

ISBN : 9789381448229 ISBN : 9789381448236 ISBN : 9789350570227 ISBN : 9789381588697 ISBN : 9788192079608 ISBN : 9789350571644 ISBN : 9789381588734 ISBN : 9789350570180 ISBN : 9789381448168

ISBN : 9789381588314 ISBN : 9789381588260 ISBN : 9788192079691 ISBN : 9789381588291 ISBN : 9789381588956 ISBN : 9789350570852 ISBN : 9789350570906 ISBN : 9789350570838 ISBN : 9789350570883

ISBN : 9789350570845 ISBN : 9789350570890 ISBN : 9789350570869 ISBN : 9789350570913 ISBN : 9789350570821 ISBN : 9783950570876 ISBN : 9789350570920 ISBN : 9789350570937

ISBN : 9789381588987 ISBN : 9789350570005 ISBN : 9789350570012 ISBN : 9789350570029 ISBN : 9789381588994 ISBN : 9789350570036 ISBN : 9789350570043 ISBN : 9789350570050 ISBN : 9789381588406 ISBN : 9789350571552

ISBN : 9789381448182 ISBN : 9789381448199 ISBN : 9789381448144 ISBN : 9789381384404 ISBN : 9789381588451 ISBN : 9789381588581 ISBN : 9789381588529 ISBN : 9789381448137 ISBN : 9789381448106 ISBN : 9789381588178

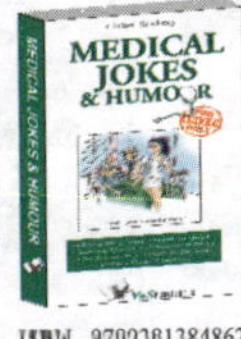

ISBN : 9789381448175 ISBN : 9789381448113 ISBN : 9789381448120 ISBN : 9789381448151 ISBN : 9789381384701 ISBN : 9789381384718 ISBN : 9789381384862 ISBN : 9788192079615 ISBN : 9789381384015 ISBN : 9789381588185

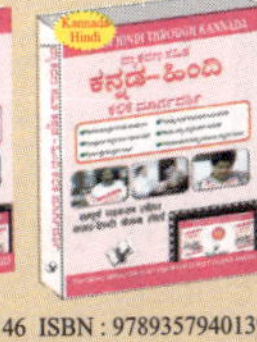

ISBN : 9789350570760 ISBN : 9789350570098 ISBN : 9789350571699 ISBN : 9789350571125 ISBN : 9789357940146 ISBN : 9789357940139 ISBN : 9789350571620 ISBN : 9789350571118 ISBN : 9789350570982 ISBN : 9789350571835

HEALTH & BEAUTY CARE/FAMILY & RELATIONS/LIFESTYLE

ISBN : 9789350570463 ISBN : 9789381588482 ISBN : 9789381448724 ISBN : 9789381448762 ISBN : 9789381448823 ISBN : 9789381384961 ISBN : 9789381384442 ISBN : 9789381448496 ISBN : 9789381588918

ISBN : 9788122307511 ISBN : 9789381448502 ISBN : 9789381384633 ISBN : 9789381448489 ISBN : 9789381384251 ISBN : 9789350570593 ISBN : 9789381384831 ISBN : 9789381384800 ISBN : 9789350570616

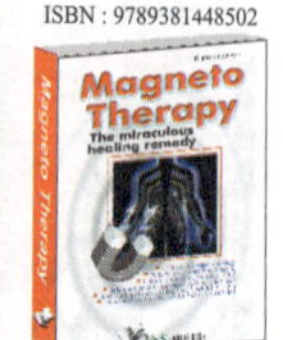

ISBN : 9789381384220 ISBN : 9789381384817 ISBN : 9789381384572 ISBN : 9789381448694 ISBN : 9789381384824 ISBN : 9789381384565 ISBN : 9789381384909 ISBN : 9789350570609 ISBN : 9789381448663

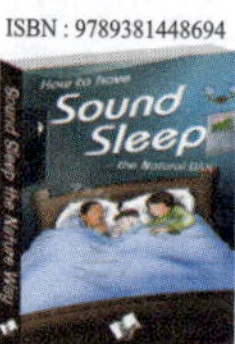

ISBN : 9789381448458 ISBN : 9789381384589 ISBN : 9788192079653 ISBN : 9789381384978 ISBN : 9789381448472 ISBN : 9789381448731 ISBN : 9789350571897 ISBN : 9789381448434 ISBN : 9789381448465

(also available in Hindi)

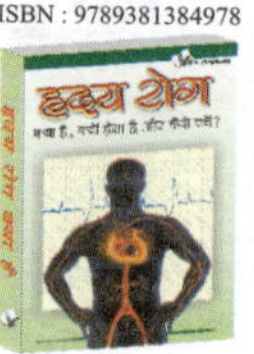

ISBN : 9789381384244 ISBN : 9789381384237 ISBN : 9789381384626 ISBN : 9789381448519 ISBN : 9789381384619 ISBN : 9789381448892 ISBN : 9789381384602 ISBN : 9789381588369 ISBN : 9789381588376

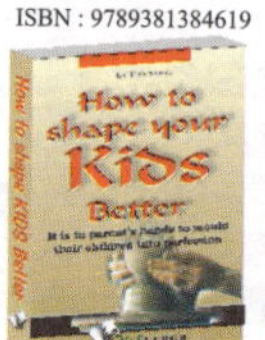

ISBN : 9789381588383 ISBN : 9789381588390 ISBN : 9789381448557 ISBN : 9789381588826 ISBN : 9789381384268 ISBN : 9788122305159 ISBN : 9789381448748 ISBN : 9789381384992 ISBN : 9789381384664

ISBN : 9789381448700 ISBN : 9789381588758 ISBN : 9789381384923 ISBN : 9789350570104 ISBN : 9789381448618 ISBN : 9789381448441 ISBN : 9789381384688 ISBN : 9789381384282 ISBN : 9788122308808

ISBN : 9789381448854 ISBN : 9789381384046 ISBN : 9789381384275 ISBN : 9789381384985 ISBN : 9789381448601 ISBN : 9789381448861 ISBN : 9789381384640 ISBN : 9789381384848 ISBN : 9789381384657

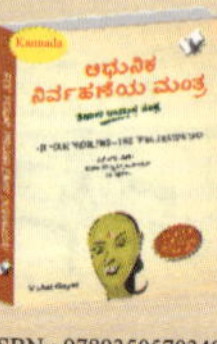

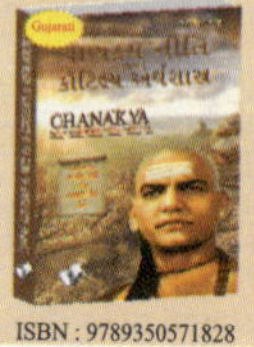

ISBN : 9788122310924 ISBN : 9789357940078 ISBN 9789350570357 ISBN : 9789350571200 ISBN : 9789350570340 ISBN : 9789350570944 ISBN : 9789350570951 ISBN : 9789350571309 ISBN : 9789350571828 ISBN : 9789350571781

SUBJECT DICTIONARIES/IELTS/ACADEMIC/COMPUTER LEARNING

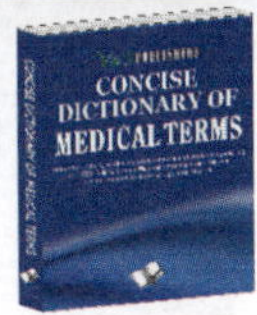

ISBN : 9789350571576
ISBN : 9789350571583
ISBN : 9789350571606
ISBN : 9789350571590
ISBN : 9789350571613
ISBN : 9789381588611 ISBN : 9789381588628 ISBN : 9789381588642 ISBN : 9789381588635 ISBN : 9789381588833 ISBN : 9789350570326 ISBN : 9789350570319 ISBN : 9789350570333

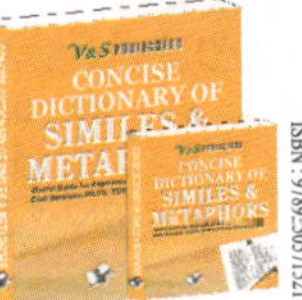

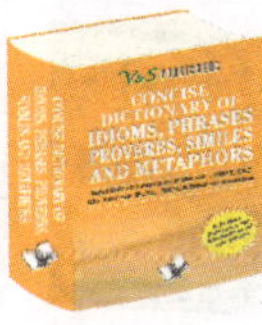

ISBN : 9789350571507
ISBN : 9789350571491
ISBN : 9789350571521
ISBN : 9789350571453
ISBN : 9789350571224 ISBN : 9789350571231 ISBN : 9789350571460 ISBN : 9789350571453 ISBN : 9789350571484 ISBN : 9789350571477 ISBN : 9789350571668 ISBN : 9789350571538

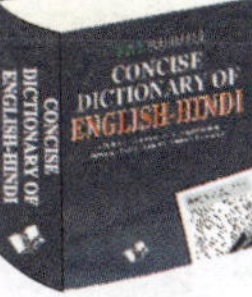

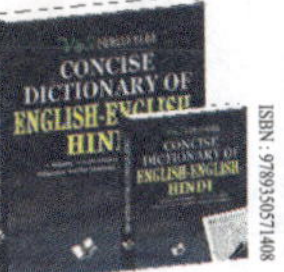

ISBN : 9789350571392
ISBN : 9789350571385
ISBN : 9789350571408
ISBN : 9789350571330
ISBN : 9789350571347
ISBN : 9789350571415 ISBN : 9789350571439 ISBN : 9789350571422 ISBN : 9789350571361 ISBN : 9789350571354 ISBN : 9789350571378 ISBN : 9789350571149 ISBN : 9789350571330

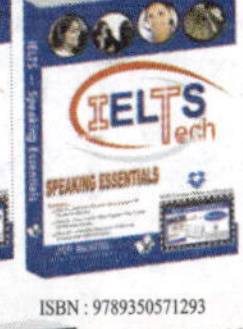

ISBN : 9789350571651 ISBN : 9789350571286 ISBN : 9789350571255 ISBN : 9789350571262 ISBN : 9789350571293 ISBN : 9789350571279 ISBN : 9789350571569 ISBN : 9789357940368 ISBN : 9789350571934

ISBN : 9789357942232

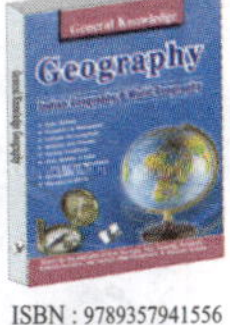

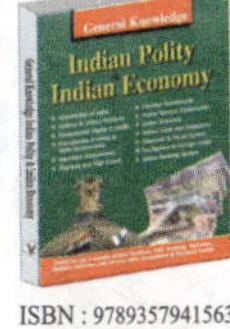

ISBN : 9789357942379
ISBN : 9789357942256
ISBN : 9789350571705 ISBN : 9789350570241 ISBN : 9789350570234 ISBN : 9789350571965 ISBN : 9789357941365 ISBN : 9789357941549 ISBN : 9789357941556 ISBN : 9789357941563 ISBN : 9789357941570

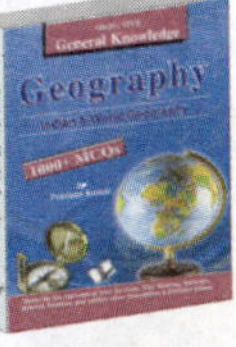

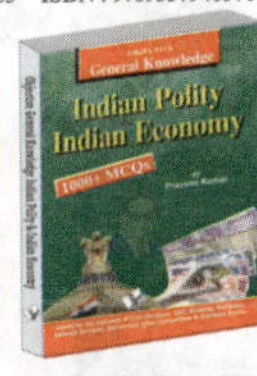

ISBN : 9789357942386
ISBN : 9789357942249
ISBN : 9789357941501 ISBN : 9789357941518 ISBN : 9789357941525 ISBN : 9789357941532 ISBN : 9789357941747 ISBN : 9789357941716 ISBN : 9789357941709 ISBN : 9789357941723

ISBN : 9789357942393
ISBN : 9789357942225
ISBN : 9789357941730 ISBN : 9789350571693 ISBN : 9789357941655 ISBN : 9789357941662 ISBN : 9789357941679 ISBN : 9789357941686 ISBN : 9789350570173 ISBN : 9789381588895

ISBN : 9789350570142 ISBN : 9789381588536 ISBN : 9789350570159 ISBN : 9789350570128 ISBN : 9789350571316 ISBN : 9789350571989 ISBN : 9789350570135 ISBN : 9789350570166
ISBN : 9789357942362

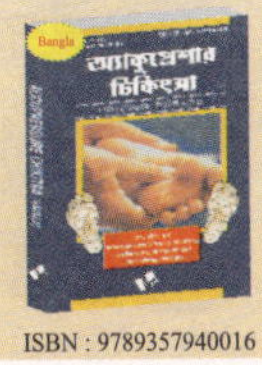

ISBN : 9789357940054 ISBN : 9789357940016 ISBN : 9789357940023 ISBN : 9789357940085 ISBN : 9789357940825 ISBN : 9789357940092 ISBN : 9789357940009 ISBN : 9789357940030 ISBN : 9789357940061

ASTROLOGY/PALMISTRY/VAASTU/HYPNOTISM/RELIGION & SPIRITUALITY

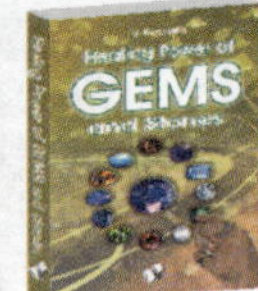

ISBN : 9789381588925 ISBN : 9789381588710 ISBN : 9789381448540 ISBN : 9789381448045 ISBN : 9789381384350 ISBN : 9789381384367 ISBN : 9789381384077 ISBN : 9789357940832 ISBN : 9789381384534

ISBN : 9789381384374 ISBN : 9789350571194 ISBN : 9789381384466 ISBN : 9789381448021 ISBN : 9789381448014 ISBN : 9789381588796 ISBN : 9789381588796 ISBN : 9789381384084 ISBN : 9789381448212

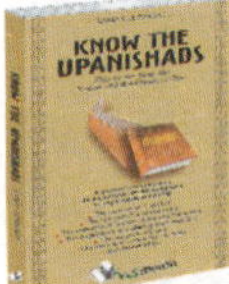

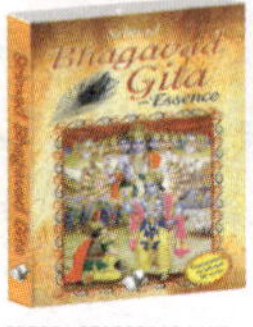

ISBN : 9789381384756 ISBN : 9789381384879 ISBN : 9788122309973 ISBN : 9788122310849 ISBN : 9789381384497 ISBN : 9789381384886 ISBN : 9789381384497 ISBN : 9789381448878 ISBN : 9789381384725

NEW ARRIVALS

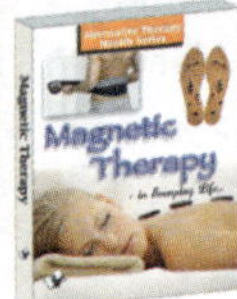

ISBN : 9789357941471 ISBN : 9789357941457 ISBN : 9789357941419 ISBN : 9789357941433 ISBN : 9789357941464 ISBN : 9789357941402 ISBN : 9789357941396 ISBN : 9789357941389 ISBN : 9789357941372 ISBN : 9789357941488

ISBN : 9789357941440 ISBN : 9789350571842 ISBN : 9789350571859 ISBN : 9789357942843 ISBN : 9789357941938 ISBN : 9789350571958 ISBN : 9789350571941 ISBN : 9789350571132 ISBN : 9789350571767 ISBN : 9789350571774

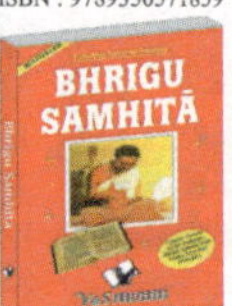
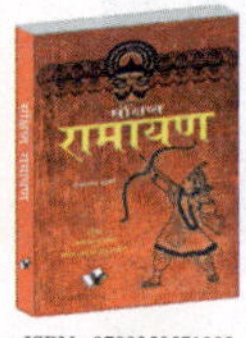

ISBN : 9789350571750 ISBN : 9789357941426 ISBN : 9789357941860 ISBN : 9789350571903 ISBN : 9789350571910 ISBN : 9789357940207 ISBN : 9789357940214 ISBN : 9789357940221 ISBN : 9789350571972 ISBN : 9789357940177

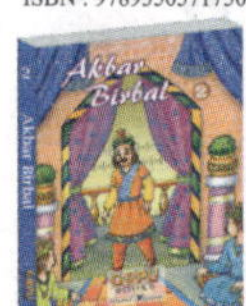

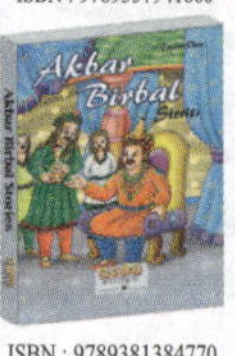

ISBN : 9789357940184 ISBN : 9789357940191 ISBN : 9789381384770 ISBN : 9789357942850 ISBN : 9789357941983 ISBN : 9789357941990 ISBN : 9789357940313 ISBN : 9789357940320 ISBN : 9789357941976 ISBN : 9789357941969

ISBN : 9789357940306
ISBN : 9789357940269

ISBN : 9789357940276
ISBN : 9789357940238

ISBN : 9789357940283
ISBN : 9789357940245

ISBN : 9789357940290
ISBN : 9789357940252

ISBN : 9789350571873
ISBN : 9789357941952

ISBN : 9789350571866
ISBN : 9789357941945

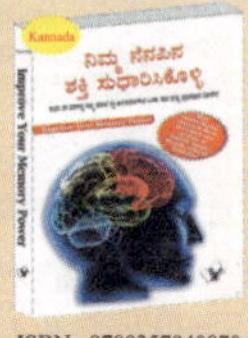

ISBN : 9789357940047 ISBN : 9789350571811 ISBN : 9789350571804 ISBN : 9789381384138 ISBN : 9789381384121 ISBN : 9789357940870 ISBN : 9789350571798 ISBN : 9789357940863 ISBN : 9789357942409